THE
CORONATION STREET
COOKBOOK

XMAS 1992

Dear Eleanor:
Isn't this fun!!

All my love always
xoxo

THE
CORONATION STREET
COOKBOOK

Graham Carlisle

VERMILION
LONDON

Acknowledgements
Anne Mackinnon, Marvin Close, Jan McVerry, Jean Halliwell, Sue Steele, Selene Preece,
Hazel Canning-Smith, Sheila Gibbons, Helen Pontin, Jan Freeman, Beryl Evans, Steve Evans,
Carolyn Reynolds, Daran Little.

Published in 1992 by Vermilion
an imprint of Ebury Press
Random House
20 Vauxhall Bridge Road
London SW1V 2SA

A catalogue record for this book is available from the British Library.

ISBN 0 09 175385 6

Edited and designed by Toucan Books Limited, London

Printed and bound by Butler and Tanner Ltd, Frome and London

CONTENTS

INTRODUCTION

I HAVE BEEN A FAN OF THE STREET since it began, and remember watching it with my Mum and Dad from a very early age. I have to admit it was 'with supper on knees', Mondays and Wednesdays (no Fridays in those days). And that was my introduction to the greatest soap ever told.

I was brought up in Bury, so there was an immediate affinity with the characters, their lifestyles and humour. And when I would hear Albert Tatlock say 'I'm off to Bury Market' — no doubt for some black puddings, which to this day I think are the best in the world — I would think, 'I go shopping there with my Mum too'.

It's not like real life, The Street, but there are parts of it that touch us all.

The collection of recipes in this long-awaited volume seem very honest and sound totally authentic. Jack and Vera's meat and potato (tatie) pie is identical to my mother's — but we always had pickled red cabbage with ours.

Being an offal fan, I am drawn to Alf's repertoire, though I have to say I prefer more Continental versions of tripe than the traditional Northern standby with milky white sauce. I hope Alf won't mind my saying this. But I bet Audrey hates the stuff. She would wish for something much more sophisticated. However, Alf's other selections are a fine bunch — particularly the black pudding and the oxtail.

Like Mavis, I am a big fan of parsnips, and I find myself wolfing down plenty when I cook them at Bibendum — but without their apparently strange qualities having the slightest effect on me...

Betty is obviously the queen of cooks on The Street, and, for me, has chosen a real *tour de force* of memorable Northern fare. Baked custard and cheese and onion tart have both appeared at Bibendum.

These are all fond memories of growing up in Lancashire. You just *know* that one of these superb dishes, cooked by Betty, would be a real treat.

I find it difficult to put my finger on the reason why Coronation Street has hooked me virtually all my life. The remarkable acting, of course, and the strong story lines. And, it has to be said, some of the gems that Bet and Rita are given to say are pure bliss.

Institution? Yes. But I do believe that Coronation Street should go down in history as one of our living national treasures.

Simon Hopkinson
Chef
Bibendum, London

BETTY'S BASICS

CONVERSION TABLES

Here are tables with the conversions that I use when I'm cooking. They might be slightly different to those in other cookery books, but I find that they work very well for these recipes.

Weight

Imperial	Metric
1/4oz	7-8g
1/2oz	15g
3/4oz	20g
1oz	30g
2oz	55g
3oz	85g
4oz (1/4lb)	110g
5oz	140g
6oz	170g
7oz	200g
8oz (1/2lb)	225g
9oz	255g
10oz	285g
11oz	310g
12oz (3/4lb)	340g
13oz	370g
14oz	400g
15oz	425g
16oz (1lb)	450g
1 1/4lb	560g
1 1/2lb	675g
2lb	900g
3lb	1.35kg
4lb	1.8kg
5lb	2.3kg
6lb	2.7kg
7lb	3.2kg
8lb	3.6kg
9lb	4.0kg
10lb	4.5kg

Liquids

Imperial	ml	fl oz
1 teaspoon	5	
1 tablespoon	15	1/2
1/4 pint	150	5
1/3 pint	190	6.6
1/2 pint	290	10
3/4 pint	425	15
1 pint	570	20
1 3/4 pint	1000 (1 litre)	35

Oven Temperatures

°C	°F	gas mark
70	150	1/4
80	175	1/4
100	200	1/2
110	225	1/2
130	250	1
140	275	1
150	300	2
170	325	3
180	350	4
190	375	5
200	400	6
220	425	7
230	450	8
240	475	8
250	500	9
270	525	9
290	550	9

Lengths

Imperial	Metric
1/2in	1cm
1in	2.5cm
2in	5cm
6in	15cm
12in	30cm

Whatever she's doing, Betty thinks it's a good idea to stop and have a cuppa every so often.

APART FROM WHEN you're baking, don't worry too much about getting very exact weights and measurements. You know how many carrots you want to eat or how big a chop you can afford and that's the amount you'll use. Also, most recipes like casseroles and the like are distinctly moveable feasts. If you haven't got one particular ingredient try sticking in what you have got that's in the same line. You'll be unlucky if it doesn't work.

SHORTCRUST PASTRY

Enough to line an 8 inch/20cm pie dish
4OZ/110G FLOUR
2OZ/55G MARGARINE (OR A MIXTURE OF MARGARINE AND LARD)
PINCH OF SALT
3 TABLESPOONS/45ML WATER

1. Sieve the flour and salt into a bowl.
2. Cut the margarine into cubes and add to the flour. Using your fingertips, rub the flour into the fat until it looks crumbly all over.
3. Add the cold water a bit at a time and cut and mix through with a table knife so it forms large lumps.
4. Flour your hands and gather the large lumps to form one large ball. The pastry should come away from the bowl cleanly. If it doesn't, add a little bit more water.
5. Wrap the pastry in polythene and stick in the fridge to rest it for 20-30 minutes. This is really important. You can leave it in the fridge for up to 24 hours before using it.

Note: If you are making larger quantities of pastry, stick to the formula of half as much fat to flour.

STOCKS

You can use stock cubes if you have to but none of them taste as good as home-made stock, which is very cheap and very easy to make. Whenever you buy some meat ask the butcher for a few beef bones. These will only cost a few pennies. When you have a chicken don't throw away the bones. They're precious. Use the bones to make stock. The stock will keep in the fridge for about 3 days, or you can freeze the stock and use it wherever you'd normally use a stock cube. You'll definitely notice the improvement in taste.

BEEF STOCK

Buy a few pennyworth of beef bones from the butcher. Run them under the tap to clean them. Roast the bones in a roasting tin in a hot oven for 25 minutes to brown them. Put them in a big pan with an onion, carrots and any other vegetable trimmings that are available. Leave the skin on the onion. Cover well with water and simmer gently for 2-3 hours. If the liquid gets too low, top it up with water. Don't add any salt.

Let the stock cool a little and then strain it into a clean container. When the liquid is cold cover it and put it somewhere cool or in the fridge overnight. The next day all the fat will have come to the surface and you can lift it off. You can then use the stock straight away or freeze it in small quantities for future use.

CHICKEN STOCK

If you've had a chicken, use the bones to make chicken stock exactly as you make beef stock. If you want a clear stock rather than a dark one, don't roast the bones before you add the water and vegetables.

If you haven't got any stock made and have bought a chicken, you can make some giblet stock like in Rita's Lemon Chicken on page 37.

When you've finished eating the chicken use the bones to make stock for another time.

SAUCES

If you learn how to make these two easy flour-based and cream-based sauces you can do all the recipes in this book.

A sauce is just a thickened liquid that you serve as a gravy or use as the basis for another dish such as a pie. The liquid can be flavoured with all kinds of things. If it's a savoury sauce it might be onion, cheese or mushrooms. Anything you like. But basically it's a white sauce.

WHITE SAUCE

2OZ/55G BUTTER
1 1/2OZ/45G PLAIN FLOUR
1 PINT/570ML MILK (OR A MIXTURE OF MILK AND STOCK)
SALT AND PEPPER

1. Melt the butter in a pan. Don't let it go brown.
2. Take the pan off the heat and add the flour. Stir to mix.
3. Put the pan back on the heat and add the liquid bit by bit while you continue stirring with a wooden spoon.
4. You shouldn't get any lumps if you keep stirring but if you do, press them into the side of the pan with the spoon and then scrape them off. If this doesn't work, use a metal whisk or sieve the final sauce.
5. Turn the heat down low and keep stirring as the sauce cooks and thickens. This should take between 6 and 10 minutes.
6. Taste the sauce and add salt and pepper as needed.
7. If you add 2oz/55g grated Lancashire cheese you've got a cheese sauce.

ONION CREAM SAUCE

1 ONION
1OZ/30G BUTTER
1 PINT/570ML STOCK
1 BAY LEAF
SALT AND PEPPER
1/2 SMALL CARTON OF DOUBLE CREAM (USE THE OTHER HALF ON A DESSERT)

1. Chop the onion finely.
2. Cook it gently in the butter. Don't let it brown.
3. Add the stock, bay leaf and pepper.
4. Simmer for 10-15 minutes.
5. Add the cream and simmer for another couple of minutes.
6. Taste and add seasoning as required.

You can use a leek instead of the onion for a leek sauce, or use mushrooms. Don't be afraid to add a little of something to a sauce to see what it ends up tasting like. You could add a chopped mushroom or a squirt of tomato purée to the onion sauce and it would be different but wonderful.

Above all, whatever you're cooking, do it confidently. You're in charge, not the recipe!

DEREK AND MAVIS

Whether they're eating out or eating in, Derek and Mavis always pay close attention to their food.

DEREK AND I have always been very keen on cooking. It's one of the sharing activities we do together and we're very lucky to have such similar tastes. Derek always says you can tell an awful lot about people by looking at what they eat and I'm sure he's right. Sometimes I think we must have been destined to marry each other because Derek cares just as passionately as I do about the environment and the world we live in. We often eat vegetarian. Derek says this is our way of making a statement and I'm sure this is true. We also eat meat, but that's just because we like it.

MAVIS'S PARSNIP SURPRISE

I didn't know it would cause such trouble when I read in a magazine that parsnips are an aphrodisiac, but it did seem to work. Unfortunately, I think I overdid it a bit, but I'd recommend just having the one parsnip meal to anybody. If you have any more it's at your own risk.

Serves 4
8OZ/225G CASHEW NUTS
4OZ/110G BREADCRUMBS
1 EGG, BEATEN
3 MEDIUM PARSNIPS, PEELED AND CUT INTO CHUNKS
PINCH OF MIXED HERBS
1 ONION, CHOPPED
2 CLOVES GARLIC, CRUSHED

2OZ/55G BUTTER
1/4 PINT/150ML VEGETABLE STOCK
1 TEASPOON/5ML MARMITE
8OZ/225G MUSHROOMS, WASHED AND SLICED

1. Preheat the oven to 180°C/350°F/gas mark 4.
2. Grind the nuts and mix with the breadcrumbs and egg.
3. Boil the parsnips for 10 minutes, or until just cooked. Mash them and add to the nut mixture with the herbs.
4. Gently fry the onion and crushed garlic in half the butter, then add the stock and Marmite. Add to the mixture.
5. Sauté the mushrooms in the remaining butter.
6. Grease a 2lb/900g loaf tin. Put in half of the mixture, then a layer of mushrooms, then the rest of the mixture.
7. Cover with foil and bake for 1 hour. Let it stand for 10 minutes and serve with tomato sauce.

Mavis hopefully bracing herself for any aphrodisiac effect that the Parsnip Surprise might have on Derek.

ONION TART

Serves 4
8OZ/225G SHORTCRUST PASTRY (SEE PAGE 10)
1/2 TEASPOON/2.5ML DRY MUSTARD
1 1/2LB/675G ONIONS, FINELY CHOPPED
2OZ/55G BUTTER
2OZ/55G GRATED LANCASHIRE CHEESE
2 EGGS
4 FL OZ/110ML MILK

1. Make the pastry following Betty's recipe but add 1/2 teaspoon/2.5ml dry mustard with the flour. Put the pastry in the fridge for at least half an hour.
2. Melt the butter in a pan and add the onions. Cook very slowly until they turn deep brown. Keep stirring them.
3. Preheat the oven to 180°C/350°F/gas mark 4.
4. Roll out the pastry and line a greased 8 inch/20cm flan tin with it.
5. Prick the pastry with a fork and bake blind (cover the pastry with foil and weigh down with dried beans) for 15 minutes. Remove the foil and beans. Brush the pastry with some beaten egg and bake for another 5 minutes.
6. Spread the onions over the flan base. Mix the beaten eggs with milk, salt and pepper and pour over the onions.
7. Sprinkle with the cheese and bake for 30 minutes until the tart is golden brown.

Above: One of nature's philosophers, Derek's unusual mind is always invigorated by a good cup of tea.

Left: It might sound very French but Mavis's recipe ensures that Onion Tart feels at home in Weatherfield.

DEREK AND MAVIS WILTON

DEREK AND MAVIS are nothing if not cautious. They spent twelve years courting one another – and then they were so unsure about getting married that they managed to jilt one another at the altar. They successfully tied the knot at the second attempt, and now live at No. 1 Coronation Street.

For years, Mavis has worked for Rita in The Kabin, while Derek has gone through a succession of selling jobs. In his time he has sold everything from paper products to novelty jokes. But Derek is basically a dreamer and doesn't stick at anything for long. They have tried working together in The Kabin, but Derek did not particularly enjoy his role as Mavis's assistant. In the end they are better wedding partners than they are workmates.

Though basically a timid soul, Mavis has aroused heavy passions in her time. Old beau Victor Pendlebury pursued her even after she got married – he employed Derek as a ruse to get nearer to Mavis. But this ended in tears after Victor sacked Derek.

Derek has had lots of other misfortunes. His first marriage to Angela ended messily, with poor old Mavis nearly being cited as co-respondent. And believing the myth that parsnips are an aphrodisiac nearly led to a confrontation with an angry husband who misinterpreted Derek's innocent approaches to his wife.

It didn't matter how good the food was, Rita was still not amused by Derek and Mavis's suggestion that it was time she retired.

BARBECUE HINTS FROM DEREK

BARBECUES AREN'T AS EASY as they look to the uninitiated. Mavis and I have had a fair bit of experience by now and I think I can definitely speak with authority. It's no use trying to cater with delicacy for civilized people. For a start, there aren't many civilized people around here, and once you put them anywhere near a barbecue they turn into animals. I think it's something to do with the flames. There's something quite elemental about fire that affects people's brains. All they want to do is drink vast quantities of alcohol and stuff food into their mouths. Any food will usually do as long as it's hot and can be held in one hand, thus freeing the other hand to hold a glass.

Keep it simple. Anything complicated will be wasted, so don't bother. Start the fire earlier than you think is sensible and it might just be ready to start cooking things when people begin complaining that they're hungry.

There will be no shortage of helpers, all labouring under the illusion that you are doing everything wrong. It's best to be firm with them from the start and lay down the rules clearly and simply. You are in charge. You are the chef. They are not to touch anything without instructions from you. Once you've got the ground rules sorted out you should be fine with these few simple but tasty recipes.

SWEET AND SOUR CHOPS

I SMALL LAMB CHOP PER PERSON
SALT AND PEPPER
MUSTARD
SUGAR

1. Dust the lamb chops with salt and pepper.
2. Smear one side with mustard and sprinkle with sugar.
3. Barbecue the chops on one side, then turn over, repeat the mustard and sugar coating, and finish cooking.

CHICKEN WINGS

Chicken wings are very good for barbecues as they're easy to eat when you're trying to balance a plate and a glass. Just sprinkle with salt and pepper and brush with a little oil. Put under the grill, or barbecue, until golden brown.

HONEY-BARBECUED CHICKEN

Mix some honey with a little warm water and brush the chicken pieces with it before putting them on the barbecue. Keep brushing the chicken as it cooks.

GREEN SALAD

Serves 4-6
I LETTUCE, WASHED AND TORN INTO PIECES
1/2 CUCUMBER, SLICED
2 OR 3 SPRING ONIONS, CHOPPED
FOR THE DRESSING:
6 TABLESPOONS/90ML OLIVE OIL
PINCH OF SUGAR
CHOPPED HERBS, FRESH OR DRY, ACCORDING TO WHAT'S
AVAILABLE
I TEASPOON/5ML DRY MUSTARD
SALT AND PEPPER
I TABLESPOON/15ML WINE VINEGAR

1. Put the lettuce, cucumber and spring onions into a large bowl.
2. Make a salad dressing by putting the olive oil in a screw-top jar with the sugar, mustard, herbs, salt and pepper and wine vinegar. Shake the jar to mix all the ingredients.
3. Put the dressing on the salad just before you serve it, or serve the dressing separately.

One of the world's great barbecue chefs, Derek makes sure he's dressed correctly for the job as it helps to enhance his natural authority when dealing with troublesome guests.

BET AND ALEC COOKING WITH BOOZE

When in doubt, Bet advises you to add a drop more!

ALEC: Cooking's never really been one of my strong points, but I do like to encourage other people into taking an interest in it, especially when they use the booze they're kind enough to buy from the Rovers.

However, I have dabbled in the kitchen arts from time to time, and if I say so myself it's not as difficult as some people make it out to be. Particularly that Betty Turpin. Let's face it, if you'd made as many hotpots as she has you'd be able to make them in your sleep! I've been too generous by half in my employment practices. Anybody else would have got one of these job creation kids to do the catering, but muggings here carries on supporting half the neighbourhood.

But you don't want to listen to me moaning. Here's one or two little recipes that me and Bet have made over the years, and if you fancy making them don't forget you can get all you need in the alcohol line down the Rovers Return. Good health!

BET: When he says me and Bet have made these recipes over the years he really means I've made them and he's eaten them. The only time he takes any real interest is when I tell him something's got booze in it. He then chews a bit, purses his lips and nods wisely, as though he can tell something of deep significance. It's always the same. But I can tell he enjoys it because he always wants seconds. So, if you're after getting your hubby interested in his food, serve him one of these. He'll love it.

BEEF IN BEER

Serves 4
1OZ/30G FLOUR
SALT AND PEPPER
1¹/2LB/675G STEWING STEAK, CUT INTO BITE-SIZE CHUNKS
2OZ/55G BUTTER
1 LARGE ONION, CHOPPED
1 LARGE CARROT, SLICED
4OZ/110G MUSHROOMS, WASHED AND SLICED
1 TABLESPOON/15ML SUGAR
A PINCH OF DRY MUSTARD
¹/2 PINT/290ML BEER
¹/2 PINT/290ML BEEF STOCK (SEE PAGE 10)

1. Preheat the oven to 170°C/325°F/gas mark 3.
2. Put the flour and salt and pepper into a paper bag.
3. Put the chunks of steak into the paper bag and shake it to coat the pieces.
4. In a large flame-proof casserole, melt the butter and brown the meat in it, a few pieces at a time.
5. Add the onion, carrot, mushrooms, sugar and mustard.
6. Add the beer and stock and bring to the boil.
7. Cover and bake in the oven for 1¹/2-2 hours.
8. Serve with mashed potatoes and green vegetables.

Nothing enhances the flavour of good beef more than good beer.

Alec doesn't mind testing the beer but prefers a drop of Irish given the choice.

PORK CHOPS IN CIDER

Serves 2

2 TEASPOONS/10ML OIL

1OZ/30G BUTTER

2 PORK CHOPS

1 LARGE ONION

2 DESSERT APPLES

SALT AND PEPPER

PINCH OF DRIED HERBS

2 CUPS CIDER

1 TABLESPOON/15ML DOUBLE CREAM

1. Preheat the oven to 180°C/350°F/gas mark 4.

2. Heat the oil and butter in a frying pan and brown both sides of the chops. Arrange in a casserole dish.

3. Slice the onion and peel and chop the apples. Fry together in the frying pan until the onion is soft. Keep stirring them while this is happening. Arrange the apple and onion over the chops.

4. Sprinkle salt, pepper and herbs over the chops and pour in enough cider to cover the chops.

5. Cover the dish and bake for 45 minutes.

6. Put the chops on 2 plates. Stir the cream into the liquid in the casserole and spoon over the chops.

ALEC'S WHISKEY CHICKEN

Serves 2

4 BONED CHICKEN THIGHS, CUT INTO LARGE CHUNKS
SALT AND PEPPER
1OZ/30G BUTTER
1 LARGE ONION, CHOPPED
GOOD MEASURE OF IRISH WHISKEY
4OZ/110G MUSHROOMS, WASHED AND CHOPPED
1 CARROT, PEELED AND SLICED
3/4 PINT/425ML CHICKEN STOCK (SEE PAGE 10)
SMALL CARTON OF DOUBLE CREAM

1. Preheat the oven to 200°C/400°F/gas mark 6.

2. Season the chunks of chicken with salt and pepper.

3. Seal the chicken quickly in the butter, then add the chopped onion and stir round to soften.

4. Pour over the whiskey and let it warm, then light it and shake the pan over the heat until the flames die down.

5. Add the mushrooms, carrot and the chicken stock.

6. Cover and bake in the oven for 45 minutes.

7. Add the double cream for the last 10 minutes.

8. Adjust the seasoning and serve with potatoes or rice.

DRUNKEN PIG

Serves 2

12-14OZ/340-400G PORK FILLET, CHOPPED INTO CHUNKS
SALT AND PEPPER
1 LARGE ONION
1OZ/30G BUTTER
1/2 PINT/290ML DRY WHITE WINE
1 SMALL TIN OF CHOPPED TOMATOES
2OZ/55G SLICED MUSHROOMS
1 BAY LEAF
PINCH OF DRIED THYME
FRESH PARSLEY

1. Season the chunks of pork fillet with salt and pepper.

2. Gently fry the onion in the butter and put to one side.

3. Brown the pork quickly.

4. Return the onion to the pan, add the wine and bring to the boil for 2-3 minutes.

5. Add the rest of the ingredients and simmer for 30 minutes.

6. Taste and adjust the seasoning if necessary.

7. Sprinkle with chopped parsley and serve with pasta.

Vicky Arden, Alec's granddaughter, came to live with Bet and Alec after her parents were killed in a car accident.

BET AND ALEC GILROY

THE HOSTESS WITH THE MOSTEST, Bet has been brightening up The Rovers Return bar for 21 years now. Once The Street's good-time girl, she got through a string of men friends before settling down with Alec. One of those early affairs bore her a son, Martin – but he was tragically killed in 1975. After years of working in shops and factories, Bet started off as barmaid in The Rovers under the indomitable Annie Walker. Through years of pulling pints, she developed a strong ambition to run The Rovers one day. When her dream finally came true, it led to disaster, and she ended up fleeing to Spain. But Alec chased her out there, proposed to her and brought her back into the pub as Queen of The Rovers. Since then she has presided over the comings and goings in Weatherfield's favourite pub with her own unique style.

Bet and Alec's meals are not always successful. Christmas Dinner was a very fraught occasion.

MINE HOST AT The Rovers Return, Alec gave up a life of running clubs and managing performers to marry Bet and move into Coronation Street. Once Rita Fairclough's manager, he made a name for himself in the area by opening the infamous Graffiti Club. It's always been hard for him to keep away from his 'theatrical' past, and he still yearns to get back into the business again. This has certainly led to him and Bet having their ups and downs!

Alec was married once before, to Joyce, and had a daughter called Sandra. Joyce died in 1991, and Sandra and her husband were killed in a car accident soon afterwards, leaving Alec's granddaughter Victoria orphaned. After being estranged for many years, Alec and Victoria are now together again – though Vicky spends most of the year away at private school. Alec has found the mysteries of teenage behaviour hard to fathom, but he's doing his best.

Alec will do anything to avoid spending money. Even cooking on a primus stove!

GUINNESS CASSEROLE

Serves 2
LARD OR DRIPPING
2 LARGE ONIONS
1LB/450G BRAISING STEAK, CUT INTO 4 PIECES
SEASONED FLOUR
1/2 PINT/290ML GUINNESS
1 BAY LEAF
SALT AND PEPPER

1. Preheat the oven to 150°C/300°F/gas mark 2.
2. In a flame-proof casserole, brown the chopped onions in the lard or dripping and then remove from the dish.
3. Coat the meat in seasoned flour and brown on both sides.
4. Pour the Guinness into the pan and add the onions, bay leaf, salt and pepper and bring to the boil.
5. Cover and bake for 2 1/2-3 hours.

RUM BANANAS

Serves 2
2 BANANAS
1/2OZ/15G BROWN SUGAR
1/2 TEASPOON/2.5 ML GROUND CINNAMON
1 TABLESPOON/15ML RUM
1OZ/30G BUTTER
SINGLE CREAM

1. Preheat the oven to 200°C/400°F/gas mark 6.
2. Cut a piece of foil for each banana.
3. Peel the bananas and place on the foil.
4. Sprinkle with the sugar, cinnamon and rum and dot the butter on them.
5. Fold the foil into two neat parcels and bake for 15 minutes.
6. Serve with the cream.

JACK AND VERA

TWO OF THE BEST meals you can ever have are fish and chips and meat and potato pie. The most difficult thing is to try and find them. When you think what fish and chips used to be like, it makes you weep to see what some chippies serve up. Like us, you've probably searched all over trying to find something decent. You'll probably only come up with greasy, badly cooked chips and fish coated in concrete batter. Here's how to cook your own. It'll keep you going until the world comes to its senses and everybody has access to a proper chippie.

Left: Vera isn't happy about Jack feeding his pigeon, Madonna, in the kitchen. Especially when little Tommy is about.

Far left: Despite everything Jack and Vera need each other. Like Antony and Cleopatra or Romeo and Juliet, their names will always be together.

FISH AND CHIPS

Serves 2-4

1LB/450G COD, HADDOCK OR HAKE FILLETS
1LB/450G POTATOES
LARD FOR DEEP-FRYING
FOR THE BATTER:
1 TEACUP SELF-RAISING FLOUR
1 TEACUP BEER
1 TEASPOON/5ML SALT
PEPPER

1. First make the batter. Sift the flour, salt and pepper into a bowl. Whisk in the beer gradually until the batter is smooth. Put to one side.

2. Peel the potatoes and cut into chips. Put in a bowl of cold water for half an hour.

3. Dry the chips well on a tea towel.

4. Heat the lard in a chip pan and cook the chips until they're nearly cooked. Remove chips from pan.

5. Shake a little salt and pepper over the fish, dust them with flour and then dip in the batter. Fry for 6-7 minutes until golden brown. Drain the fish and keep warm.

6. Put chips back in chip pan until fully cooked and golden.

JACK AND VERA DUCKWORTH

Jack's close proximity to beer at the Rovers is accepted by Vera, because he does at least get paid for it.

EVER SINCE A YOUNG Jack swept an impressionable Vera off her feet on the fairground he worked at over 35 years ago, the Duckworths have enjoyed a rollercoaster marriage – but with many more downs than ups.

From the cash that he earns from working as cellarman at The Rovers, Jack barely has the wherewithal to pay for the basics of his life – and for him, the basics are betting on the horses, having a pint or two and feeding his pigeons. Vera is more keen to spend what little cash she earns from Bettabuys supermarket on home improvements – like the awesome stone-cladding they had put onto the house back in 1989. Her only real hobby is making regular visits to the bingo hall with her best friend Ivy.

Quick-tempered Vera sometimes finds it difficult to keep her mouth shut, and as a consequence has been sacked twice – but then re-instated – from her job at Bettabuys.

Both Jack and Vera have had their moments on the extra-marital front. After Jack had been trying it on with a barmaid at The Rovers, Vera took a pair of scissors to all his trousers and cut them to shreds. And when the two of them went away to Pwhelli for a second honeymoon, Vera stormed home early after Jack accused her of flirting with the camp entertainer.

To add to their domestic woe, only son Terry has always been a bit of a tearaway. Graduating from petty crime to assault, he's now in jail, leaving his young wife, Lisa, and son, Tom, to live with Vera and Jack.

Terry has always been a source of distress to Jack and Vera but little Tommy and Lisa have more than made up for it.

MEAT AND POTATO PIE

These days you're not supposed to call this meat and potato pie. It's supposed to be called potato and meat pie because there's more potato than meat. As though everybody doesn't already know that. There must be some idiot somewhere with nothing better to do than make daft rules all day.

When we were kids our dad used to say you got a prize if you found a piece of meat in a meat and potato pie. Well there's plenty of meat in this one.

Serves 4

2 LARGE ONIONS

1LB/450G SKIRT OR SHIN BEEF CUT INTO FAIRLY SMALL PIECES

2LB/900G POTATOES PEELED AND CUT INTO LARGE PIECES

BEEF STOCK (SEE PAGE 10) OR WATER TO COVER

SALT AND PEPPER

FOR THE PASTRY:

8OZ/225G SELF-RAISING FLOUR

1 1/2 TEASPOON/7.5ML SALT

4OZ/110G MARGARINE

1. Preheat the oven to 160°C/325°F/gas mark 3.

2. Slice the onions and put them into an ovenproof pie dish with the meat and potatoes. Add salt and pepper and pour over stock to cover. If you're using stock cubes go easy on the salt.

3. Cover and cook in the oven for 2 hours, or until the meat is tender.

4. Make the pastry by sifting flour and salt together. Rub the margarine into the flour until it resembles fine breadcrumbs. Add cold water little by little to make a firm dough.

5. Roll out the pastry so that it is approximately 1 1/2 inches thick and cover the pie with it.

6. Turn up the oven to 200°C/400°F/gas mark 6 and bake the pie for 30 minutes until the pastry is golden brown.

7. Serve with pickled beetroot.

PERCY SUGDEN

SOME OF THESE YOUNG PEOPLE today laugh at people like me when we tell them that food today isn't as good as it was. That's because they've never tasted any better. I've eaten all over the world, and I can tell you there's nothing like good Lancashire food. If you saw some of the things these foreigners eat, it'd make your hair curl.

When we were out in the desert Monty told me that my cooking was worth twenty tanks. And he was right! He always used to ask for my special gravy so I've included the recipe here along with a few of my favourites from over the years. They're not what you'd call sophisticated dishes, but if I'm not mistaken you'll get as much satisfaction as I do in making and eating them.

PERCY'S SPECIAL GRAVY

If I say so myself, this gravy is the best in the world. The secret ingredient is a drop of sherry, but there've been times when I've been glad of a drop of anything at all to put in it!

I SMALL ONION
BUTTER
PLAIN FLOUR
SHERRY
3/4 PINT/425ML BEEF STOCK (SEE PAGE 10) OR STOCK CUBE

1. Chop the onion finely and cook gently in a little butter, not letting it go brown.
2. Add a little flour and let that colour a bit. Add your beef stock bit by bit and keep stirring it. Let it simmer until it thickens and then add a drop or two of sherry to taste. Taste it and then add salt and pepper if it needs it. If you're using a stock cube, dissolve it in boiling water according to the instructions on the packet, but watch out that it isn't too salty.

Note: This will make an excellent gravy, but you can make it even better if you've cooked a roast. Lift the meat out of the roasting tin, pour off most of the fat and put the tin on top of the stove. Pour in your stock and scrape the bottom of the tin with a spoon to mix in all the tasty bits. Strain the stock through a sieve and then add it carefully to the onion and flour as above.

Left: Percy Sugden learnt to cook on the battlefields of North Africa.

BEEF AND COW HEEL PIE

Me and Mrs Bishop usually get at least two meals out of this. It's well worth the trouble to find a butcher who will do cow heel, but you definitely won't find any at Bettabuys. You'll have to go to a proper butcher's shop, and a good thing too!

Serves 4
3/4 LB/340G SHIN OF BEEF
1/2 DRESSED COW HEEL
I ONION STUCK WITH CLOVES
I PINT/570ML BEEF STOCK (SEE PAGE 10)
SALT AND PEPPER
ILB/450G SHORTCRUST PASTRY (SEE NOTE BELOW)
I EGG

1. Preheat the oven to 190°C/375°F/gas mark 5.
2. First of all you put the beef, the cow heel and the onion in a pan with the stock and a little salt and pepper. Cover the pan and simmer gently for about 3 hours.
3. When cooked take out the beef and cow heel and strip off all the meat, cutting it into I inch/2.5cm pieces.
4. Line an 8 inch/20cm pie dish with half the pastry. Fill with the meats and add a little of the stock. Cover with the rest of the pastry, make a small vent hole and brush with beaten egg or a little milk.
5. Bake for 45 minutes or until golden brown.

Note: You can use frozen shortcrust pastry for this one if you want, but better still use Betty Turpin's recipe on page 10. You can use a stock cube instead of beef stock, but it's cheaper and tastier to make your own. If you do use a cube, don't add so much salt.

PERCY'S HOTPOT

I usually make enough for me and Mrs Bishop to have two good meals out of this. This is for preference, as hotpot always tastes better the second day, though make sure you heat it through properly. My hotpot's a bit different from Betty's but no worse for that. The difference is the layer of bacon just beneath the final layer of potatoes, which I think improves the flavour.

They say that folk used to put oysters and mushrooms in hotpot. Well if they did, then it's a rare example of progress in the world, because nobody puts them in any more. Stick to the proper ingredients. If you must put a carrot in, I suppose you can, but believe me when I tell you it's twice as good without.

Serves 2
8OZ/225G SCRAG END OF NECK OF LAMB, OR 4 SMALL CHOPS
1 LARGE ONION
2LB/900G POTATOES
3/4 PINT/425ML BEEF STOCK (SEE PAGE 10)
2 OR 3 RASHERS OF BACON (SMOKED IF PREFERRED)
2OZ/55G DRIPPING OR BUTTER

1. Preheat the oven to 170°C/325°F/gas mark 3.
2. Trim and chop the neck of lamb and peel and slice the onion and potatoes. Save 1 potato and slice it thinly.
3. Layer the lamb, onion and potatoes in a casserole dish, seasoning each layer as you go along. Add the beef stock. If you're using a stock cube, remember that it'll add a bit of salt to the flavour.
4. Stretch the rashers of bacon with the back of a knife and spread out over the top of the hotpot.
5. Cover with the thinly sliced potato and dot with the dripping or butter.
6. Cover and cook in the oven for 2 hours.
7. Remove the lid and turn the oven up to 220°C/425°F/gas mark 7 for about 20 minutes or until the top is golden brown.
8. Serve with pickled beetroot or red cabbage.

APPLE DUMPLINGS

Serves 2
2 LARGE COOKING APPLES
1OZ/30G CURRANTS AND/OR RAISINS
1OZ/30G BUTTER
PINCH OF CINNAMON
GRATED RIND OF 1 LEMON
2OZ/55G BROWN SUGAR
4OZ/110G SHORTCRUST PASTRY (SEE PAGE 10)
CASTER SUGAR

1. Preheat the oven to 180°C/350°F/gas mark 4.
2. Peel and core the apples.
3. Mix together the raisins, butter, cinnamon, lemon rind and brown sugar. Stuff the mixture into the apples.
4. Roll out the pastry and cut into two circles large enough to enclose the apples.
5. Wrap each apple in a circle of pastry, moisten the edges and seal them. Put the apples on a baking tray with the sealed pastry edges underneath and bake for about 1 hour or until golden brown. Sprinkle with caster sugar.
6. Serve hot or warm with custard or cream.

PERCY'S PARADISE TRIFLE

Serves 4
1 PACKET RED JELLY
1 FROZEN CREAM CAKE
2 MEASURES OF SHERRY
1 MEASURE OF WHISKY
1 LARGE TIN PEACHES
1 TIN READY-MADE CUSTARD
1 SMALL CARTON WHIPPING CREAM
GLACÉ CHERRIES

1. Put the cream cake at the bottom of a trifle dish and pour over the sherry and whisky. Spread the peaches over the cake.
2. Make the jelly according to the instructions on the packet. Let it cool a bit and then pour over the cake to set.
3. Spread the custard over the jelly. Whip the cream until it's stiff. Spread it over the custard.
4. Decorate with glacé cherries.
5. Refrigerate until ready to serve.

PERCY SUGDEN

PERCY SERVED AS CARETAKER at the community centre before becoming long-suffering Emily's lodger in 1988. He was a memorable lollipop man before being forcibly retired. There isn't much in Percy's life that runs smoothly and he's never slow to complain about his fellow citizens' actions. He's well aware that the world has changed but he'd rather it hadn't bothered. Progress seems to be a plot invented to irritate him.

He presents to the world the image of a grumpy embittered old man but if you scratch the surface you always find that his bark is worse than his bite and that deep down he likes nothing better than sorting out his neighbours' troubles – if they'll let him!

Phyllis has pursued him with absolutely no success and if it's anything to do with him she'll never catch him, but the chase definitely keeps him on his toes.

During the war Percy drove a canteen cookhouse van around Europe, and seems to have been present at most of the important battles and campaigns. Monty certainly would have found it difficult to achieve much success without Percy's gravy.

He's very fond of his landlady, Emiy Bishop, and won't hear a word against her. Woe betide anybody Percy overhears gossiping about Mrs Bishop. His other great friend is Randy, his budgerigar.

Percy's budgie, Randy, is his greatest pal. Whenever he feels a bit down he has a little chat to Randy and then cooks himself and Emily something a bit special.

Percy's often to be found propping up the end of the bar nursing his half-pint of beer – except when he's barred and has to drink down the Legion. He's a strong believer that good British beer is a wonderful aid to the digestion.

EMILY'S AFTERNOON TEA AND CAKES

I DO ENJOY A QUIET little moment or two in the afternoon to reflect on the day's events. It's not always easy when Mr Sugden's about, but he does always mean well so I don't really mind listening to him. Sometimes I go to the café. As much for the company as anything else. If I'm at home on my own I might just have a scone and a cup of tea. If there are guests I usually add a couple of cakes. I do think it makes a difference if you take the trouble to do things properly. It really doesn't take more than a moment or two to get out side plates and proper cutlery, and it gives me a great deal of pleasure.

If you want something a little more substantial you can serve some boiled ham with bread and butter, or if you like you could try some of Ivy's potted shrimps, which I can highly recommend.

THE PERFECT POT OF TEA

It's a false economy to buy very cheap tea. Much better to spend a few extra pennies and end up with a proper cup that you really enjoy.

1. Use fresh water in the kettle. When it's boiled pour a little boiling water into the teapot and swirl it round to warm the pot.
2. Add 1 teaspoon of tea for each person. Boil the kettle again and pour the water into the teapot.
3. Stir the tea, put the lid on and cover the teapot with a tea cosy. Pour milk into the cups.
4. After 4 minutes pour the tea into the cups. Add sugar if used.

STRAWBERRY SHORTBREAD

This is suitable for a quick and easy dessert as well as for afternoon tea. Simply take some shortbread biscuits and layer them with sliced strawberries and whipped cream. If you're careful you can make two layers with three biscuits. If you serve it as a dessert, make a fruit sauce by putting a tin of strawberries through a sieve and pouring a little on to the serving plate next to the shortbread.

CHOCOLATE SANDWICH CAKE SPLIT WITH CREAM

2 LARGE EGGS
4OZ/110G BUTTER
4OZ/110G CASTER SUGAR
1OZ/30G COCOA POWDER DISSOLVED IN A LITTLE MILK
4OZ/110G FLOUR
1 TEASPOON/5ML BAKING POWDER
1 SMALL CARTON OF WHIPPING CREAM
ICING SUGAR

1. Preheat the oven to 190°C/375°F/gas mark 5.
2. Beat the eggs.
3. Cream the butter and sugar until white and fluffy.
4. Beat the eggs into the creamed butter and sugar.
5. Add the cocoa and carry on beating.
6. Fold in the sifted flour and baking powder.
7. Pour the mixture into 2 greased and lined 6-7inch/15-18cm sandwich tins. Smooth over the tops and bake for 20 minutes, or until springy to the touch.
8. Leave to cool on 2 cake racks, then whip the cream and sandwich the two halves together. Dust the top with icing sugar.

Emily always loves her afternoon tea even if she has to have it in Jim's Café to get away from Percy.

Cherry scones are a little more trouble than the ordinary ones but Emily thinks they are well worth the effort.

CHERRY SCONES

1LB/450G SELF-RAISING FLOUR
1 TEASPOON/5ML SALT
4OZ/110G BUTTER
8OZ/225G GLACÉ CHERRIES
4OZ/110G SUGAR
2 EGGS, BEATEN
5 FL OZ/150ML MILK

1. Preheat the oven to 220°C/425°F/gas mark 7.
2. Sift together the flour and salt.
3. Rub the butter into the salted flour until the mixture looks like breadcrumbs.
4. Roughly chop the cherries and add to the mixture.
5. Add the sugar and beaten eggs.
6. Gradually add the milk until the dough is smooth.
7. Knead the dough lightly and roll or press out until about 1 inch/2.5cm thick. Cut into small rounds.
8. Brush with milk or dust with flour.
9. Bake for 10 minutes or until well risen and brown.

EMILY BISHOP

A PERMANENT FIXTURE on The Street for 30 years, Emily has seen it all in Weatherfield – and despite her quiet and mild nature, a lot of it has happened to her. In 1964, she jilted her boss, Leonard Swindley, at the altar, and then married bigamist Arnold Swain. But the greatest tragedy of her life happened back in 1976, when her third husband, Ernie, was murdered in an armed raid.

Always a worker, Emily spent many years behind a counter of some form or another – but also toiled away for Mike Baldwin as a book-keeper. Since retiring, she's kept herself busy with hospital visiting and serving on various committees. For a while, she even ran the local charity shop in Coronation Street. Emily became a Christian at fifteen, and has been active in the local chapel on Mawdsley Street ever since.

Though she has no children of her own, she is very close to Deirdre Barlow and is god-mother to her daughter, Tracy.

But perhaps the thing that keeps her busiest in her retirement is coping with Percy as her lodger. She thought about moving away from Weatherfield but, thankfully, changed her mind when she realized how much she'd miss Coronation Street. Recently, Emily suffered a small breakdown and she was suddenly rather glad of Percy's presence and, indeed, friendship.

The saintly Emily Bishop is Percy's long-suffering landlady.

RITA'S SUNDAY DINNER

I'VE CHOSEN TO DO A ROAST dinner because I've always thought that if you can get through cooking and serving one without having a nervous breakdown, you can probably cope with anything. Usually everybody gets in a mess trying to time everything so it's all ready at once. If you do the vegetables like I do them here, you can't go wrong. Prepare everything in advance and there's less chance of getting in a panic.

RITA'S LEMON ROAST CHICKEN

Serves 4

1 ROASTING CHICKEN, WITH GIBLETS IF POSSIBLE
1 ONION AND 1 CARROT, FOR THE GIBLET STOCK
SALT AND PEPPER
BAY LEAF
2 LEMONS
2OZ/55G BUTTER, OR OLIVE OIL
3 RASHERS STREAKY BACON
2LB/900G POTATOES
1 TABLESPOON/15ML FLOUR
GLASS OF WHITE WINE IF YOU'VE GOT IT
2 OF THE FOLLOWING: 1¼LB/560G CARROTS; 4 LARGE
COURGETTES; 1 CAULIFLOWER; 1LB/450G BRUSSEL SPROUTS;
8OZ/225G PEAS

1. Fifteen minutes before you need it, preheat the oven to 180°C/350°F/gas mark 4.

2. Remove the giblets and put them in a saucepan with the sliced onion and peeled and chopped carrot. Add a bit of black pepper and a bay leaf and about ¾ pint/425ml water. Simmer while you roast the chicken.

3. Squeeze the juice of half a lemon over the chicken and stick the squeezed half inside the chicken. Add some salt and pepper inside the chicken and season the outside. Rub the butter over the outside of the bird or use olive oil. Cover the breast with bacon, or with some kitchen foil. This stops the breast drying out before the rest of the bird is cooked. Stick in the oven for 10 minutes, and then turn the heat down to 160°C/325°F/gas mark 3. The chicken should be roasted for another 20 minutes per pound.

4. Peel the potatoes and cut into even-sized pieces. Boil them for 5-10 minutes, then drain off the water and put the lid back on the pan and shake it. This will roughen up the outsides of the potatoes and make them crispier. Alternatively, cut partway through the potatoes as though you were making potato slices about a twopenny piece thick, but keeping them attached at one end. These roast potatoes look like roast hedgehogs and have more crispy bits. Put the potatoes in the roasting pan with the chicken, turning them in the fat, for the last 25 minutes.

5. To test if the chicken is cooked, use a sharp knife or a skewer and pierce the thickest part of the leg. If the juices run out clear it's cooked. If they are pink, return to the oven.

Rita outside The Kabin.

6. Take the chicken out of the roasting pan and put it on a warm serving plate. Leave it to rest for 15 to 20 minutes. This firms up the flesh so it's easier to carve and also gives you time to finish off the vegetables. Don't worry about it keeping warm. It'll be plenty hot enough.

7. When the potatoes are brown, drain them on kitchen paper and put them back in the oven in an ovenproof serving dish. If they're crisp enough turn the oven down, otherwise leave it up until they are crisp.

8. Angle the roasting tin so that all the fat runs into one corner. You can see the chicken juices under the fat. Spoon off as much fat as possible. Put the roasting tin on top of the oven over a flame or ring and sprinkle the flour into it. Stir it round and scrape the pan with a spoon until the flour browns. Don't worry about the burnt bits or the remains of the roast potatoes. Just keep stirring. Pour in the glass of white wine if you've got it and stir. Then add the giblet stock. Keep stirring and scraping while it thickens a bit. Add the juice of the remaining half of the lemon. Pour the lemon gravy through a sieve into a pan. Taste and add salt and pepper as needed.

9. Try to choose at least a couple of vegetables that will contrast in colour. Carrots and peas, or courgettes, sprouts and cauliflower. Take your pick. Time it so that you either cook them in simmering water or steam them after you've taken out the chicken. If you boil them, put a squeeze of lemon juice in the water. It'll help keep the vegetables' natural colour.

10. Alternatively, have a large pan of simmering water and partly cook each vegetable separately before you start cooking the chicken. Do each vegetable so that they're still very crisp. Run them under the cold tap to cool them quickly so that they stop cooking. When you want to serve them, put them back into simmering water for 1 minute.

This method is better than cooking them from scratch when you need them as it's easier and usually gets better results. It can be done a few hours in advance, making it ideal for when you've got guests and want to spend time with them instead of slaving over the stove.

11. You can carve the chicken and allow everyone to help themselves to everything, or you can serve a portion of chicken and some sauce on a plate, keeping the vegetables separate, or you can pile everything on to individual plates. Whichever way, it will be delicious. The best way to use the second lemon is to have a very large vodka and tonic just before you start the final stages of the meal.

One of the joys of making Rita's summer pudding is that it can be made well ahead of the meal. If you want to make it a bit special you can make individual ones for each person but it makes no difference to the taste. Big or small, they are delicious.

SUMMER PUDDING

Serves 4

1³/₄ LB/785G SOFT FRUIT: STRAWBERRIES, RASPBERRIES,
REDCURRANTS, BLACKCURRANTS (OR SOME OF THESE, MIXED)
4OZ/110G CASTER SUGAR
ABOUT 8 SLICES OF THIN WHITE BREAD

1. Gently cook the fruit with the sugar for 3 to 5 minutes. Reserve 1 cup of juice.

2. Butter a 1¹/₂ pint/860ml basin. Cut the crusts off the bread and line the basin carefully, overlapping the slices, pressing together the edges and reserving a slice to cover the top of the pudding.

3. Pour the fruit into the basin and cover with the remaining bread.

4. Put a saucer with a 3-4lb/1.35kg weight on top.

5. Refrigerate overnight.

6. Turn the pudding out on to a serving dish, and pour over the reserved juice to make sure the pudding is all red.

7. Serve with cream.

Note: You can use tinned soft fruit.

RITA SULLIVAN

A FORMER NIGHT CLUB singer, Rita's life has at times been as sad as some of the songs she used to sing. She gave up crooning in 1977, to marry local builder Len Fairclough. After just six years of marriage, he then died tragically in a car crash.

Three years later, Rita fell for Alan Bradley and let him move in with her. The man turned out to be an absolute monster – after trying to kill Rita, pushing her towards a nervous breakdown, and then himself serving time in prison, Bradley finally died under a tram in Blackpool. Rita had originally met Bradley through fostering his daughter, Jenny. She has another foster child, Sharon, who now lives in Sheffield.

Just to add to Rita's tragic affairs of the heart, she married her second husband, Ted Sullivan, knowing that he had a brain tumour.

But a happy constant in Rita's life for the last twenty years has been running The Kabin. First put in there to manage it by Len Fairclough, Rita ended up running and owning the little newsagent's shop – and the flat above it, where she now lives. Her long-time friend and foil in The Kabin is Mavis. Over the years she has listened and commented upon the saga of Mavis's life and times with wit and good humour, and without ever losing her patience – at least not for very long!

Perhaps because of her own misfortunes, she is a tower of strength and common sense for her neighbours in The Street and when she gets together with her friend, Bet, they make a formidable team.

Top: Mavis's logic would baffle most people, but Rita is more than used to it.
Above: Rita found brief happiness with Ted Sullivan, but it was not to last.

Randy Reg's Valentine Dinner

I THINK I CAN SAFELY SAY that I'm a man of the world. I do know how to properly impress a woman. You won't find me offering a lady half a bitter and a packet of crisps. Oh dearie me, no! You need a certain style and sophistication these days and thank God I've got it. The meal that I've planned for your delectation is guaranteed to be successful. The only reason it's never yet worked with Rita is that she's never given me the chance to make it for her. It is, of course, only a matter of time.

Each one of these delectable dishes contains ingredients that are thought to be aphrodisiacs. You may decide that it's too dangerous to eat all three at once or you may decide to go for the grand slam. Either way, don't forget to do them justice. Put on some mood music, turn the lights down low and away you go.

If you get to the end of the meal and your intended hasn't hurled herself across the table and grappled you to the floor then my name isn't Reg Holdsworth! *Bon appetit, mes chéris!*

Oh, I forgot to say. All ingredients are, of course, available from Bettabuys.

OYSTERS AND CHAMPAGNE

SEAWEED

6 OYSTERS

1 BOTTLE CHAMPAGNE

LEMON

1. Get some seaweed off the fishmonger when you buy the oysters. Arrange it as a bed on 2 plates.

2. Discard any oysters that aren't tightly closed.

3. To open the oysters use a special oyster knife or a short, stiff-bladed knife. Hold the oyster on a flat surface with the rounded half of the shell downwards. Cover it with a tea towel to protect your hand. Ease the knife into the hinge end of the oyster and move it from side to side until the shell separates. Carefully remove the top part of the shell and ease your knife under the oyster to separate it from the bottom shell.

4. Try and keep the liquid in the bottom shell as you arrange it on the seaweed. Put three on each plate.

5. Arrange some slices of lemon round the oysters.

6. To eat them, squeeze a few drops of lemon juice on to the oyster. Tip the oyster into your mouth. Wash it down with the champagne.

Here's to you and here's to me
And here's to the pretty girls
Who live by the sea.

SALMON BAKED IN PASTRY WITH GINGER

1 PACKET FROZEN PUFF PASTRY

SMALL PIECE OF GINGER ROOT

2OZ/55G BUTTER

2 SALMON FILLETS ABOUT 4OZ/110G EACH

SALT AND PEPPER

NEW POTATOES

FRENCH BEANS

1. Preheat the oven to 200°C/400°F/gas mark 6.

2. Roll out the pastry thinly and cut 2 two squares big enough to enclose the salmon when folded into parcels.

3. Peel the ginger and chop it finely. Mix it into the butter.

4. Divide the butter between the 2 pastry squares, spreading it into a square slightly bigger than the size of the salmon fillets.

5. Season the salmon and place each piece on top of the ginger butter.

6. Fold up the pastry squares like parcels.

7. Put the parcels with the joins underneath on a baking tray. Brush with a little milk.

8. Bake for 25 minutes or until golden brown. Turn the parcels over for the last 5 minutes to cook the bottom of the pastry.

9. While the salmon is baking steam a few new potatoes and a few French beans.

10. Put each salmon parcel on a plate and slice it in half down the middle. Arrange the two halves at an angle to each other so you can see inside the parcels.

11. Arrange the vegetables around the salmon and serve.

Strawberry Hearts. If you can't get to Bettabuys to buy fresh strawberries then you can use any other fruit to decorate them.

STRAWBERRY HEARTS

1 TIN OF SCOTTISH RASPBERRIES
1 CARTON OF DOUBLE CREAM
1 PUNNET OF STRAWBERRIES
ICING SUGAR

1. Save the liquid from the tin of raspberries.
2. Press the raspberries through a sieve with the back of a spoon, adding a little of the liquid to make a good pouring sauce.
3. Pour a little of the sauce on to 2 plates.
4. Hold the plates by the edges and swirl the sauce to cover the base of the plates.
5. Put a heart-shaped biscuit cutter in the middle of the plate. Whip the cream and spoon it into the cutter.
6. Slice the strawberries in half and carefully place them on and around the cream heart.
7. Remove the cutter.
8. Dust with icing sugar.

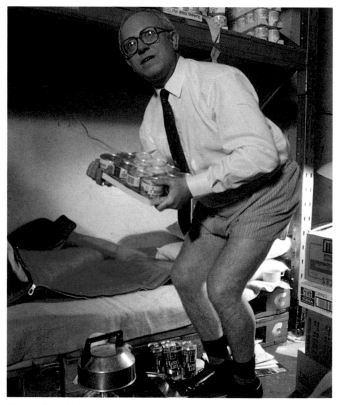

Even when he's in dire straits Reg never loses his natural style and elegance.

REG HOLDSWORTH

RANDY REG, AS HE'S KNOWN down The Street, came to Weatherfield back in 1989, to manage the local branch of Bettabuys Supermarkets plc. He likes to think of himself as something of a smooth talker, and has always had an eye for Rita Fairclough. She was mortified when he not only moved into Coronation Street but set up home next to her – water bed and all! His ex-wife wanted to put so much distance between them that she moved out to New Zealand. So far, Rita has shown herself to be more than a match for Reg, but Reg rarely let's reality impinge on his fantasies, so this has in no way dampened his ardour.

But The Street – and particularly the staff at Bettabuys – have learned to live with Reg and his little ways. Vera and Ivy regularly suffer from Reg's little foibles but the person who takes the brunt of it is his right-hand man, Curly. As a management team, Reg and Curly leave an awful to to be desired.

The store is very much Reg's kingdom, and he works hard to run a tight ship, but somehow something always goes wrong. The scourge of his life is area manager Brendan Scott, who would like nothing better than to see Reg out of a job.

Reg hasn't been able to convince Rita to sample his culinary delights yet, but he lives in hope.

BETTY'S HOTPOT

Betty's hotpot is so vital to the Rovers that when Alec made Betty redundant he had to beg her to return!

I HAVE TO ADMIT I feel a bit proud when I think how popular my hotpot has become and how many portions we must have sold in the Rovers over the years. It must be a lot, because the thought of it even puts a smile on Alec's face! Some people might think it's old-fashioned, but it's no worse for that. And if you're trying to feed a family then it's hard to beat.

I've tried out lots of fancy versions of hotpot but I always come back to this one. You can add kidneys and even oysters and mushrooms if you like them, but there's no need and I've come round to the view that in cooking the simplest way is often the best. It's certainly true with hotpot.

BETTY'S HOTPOT

Serves 4

1LB/450G SCRAG END OR BEST END NECK OF LAMB, CHOPPED
1¹/2LB/675G POTATOES, PEELED
1 LARGE ONION
SALT AND PEPPER
¹/2-³/4 PINT/290-425ML CHICKEN STOCK (SEE PAGE 10)
1OZ/30G LARD OR DRIPPING

1. Preheat the oven to 190°C/375°F/gas mark 5.

2. Fry the meat quickly to give it a good brown colour.

3. Put the meat into a casserole dish.

4. Slice the peeled potatoes and onions thinly.

5. Arrange them on top of the meat, seasoning them as you go along. Overlap the top layer of potatoes.

6. Pour in the stock.

7. Melt the lard and brush over the top of the potatoes.

8. Cover the dish and bake in the oven for at least 2 hours. Uncover the dish and turn the oven up until the top browns.

8. Serve with pickled red cabbage, pickled beetroot or chutney.

RHUBARB CHUTNEY

2LBS/900G RHUBARB
2 LEMONS
2LBS/900G DEMERARA SUGAR
PINCH OF CAYENNE PEPPER
1OZ/30G SALT
1LB/450G SULTANAS
1OZ/30G GARLIC
1 PINT/570ML MALT VINEGAR
1OZ/30G ROOT GINGER

1. Wash the rhubarb and cut it into small pieces. Put it in a bowl and squeeze the juice from the lemons on to it.

2. Put the rhubarb and lemon juice, sugar, cayenne, salt, sultanas, chopped garlic, and vinegar into a preserving pan. Bruise the ginger with the flat blade of a knife and tie in a muslin bag. Add to the mixture.

3. Simmer the mixture, stirring constantly, for 60-90 minutes until it's tender and thick. Remove the ginger.

4. Pour into clean dry jars and seal. Keep for a month before serving.

Betty's hotpot – the finest in the world!

PICKLED RED CABBAGE

2LB /900G SHREDDED RED CABBAGE
1LB/450G ONIONS
2OZ/55G COOKING SALT
FOR THE SPICED VINEGAR:
2 PINTS /1 LITRE MALT VINEGAR
2OZ/55G PICKLING SPICE

1. Put the shredded cabbage and thinly sliced onions in layers in a bowl. Sprinkle each layer with salt.

2. Cover and put in a cool place for 24 hours.

3. Meanwhile make some spiced vinegar. Add the pickling spice to the vinegar. Bring to the boil and allow to cool. Cover and leave for 2 hours. Strain before using.

4. Drain the cabbage and put into pots. Cover with cold spiced vinegar and cover pots. Store in a cool dark place for 2-3 weeks before use.

PICKLED BEETROOT

1LB /450G BEETROOT
1 PINT/590ML VINEGAR OR PICKLING VINEGAR (SEE ABOVE)

1. Cook the unpeeled beetroot in boiling salted water for 1¹/2 to 2 hours, or until tender.

2. Let the beetroot cool then peel and slice or dice.

3. Cover with cold vinegar. Leave for 24 hours before using.

BETTY'S BAKING

YOU MIGHT FIND BAKING hard work, but think yourself lucky that you haven't got Alec Gilroy breathing down your neck. Look at me. After all these years I don't suppose I should let him get to me but I still do. He's all mouth and trousers, really, but it's difficult to ignore him when he starts jumping up and down. It's a lot easier dealing with Bet, but then it would be, wouldn't it.

As regards the baking, I've just about got used to the new kitchen at the Rovers and I must admit it's a big improvement on the old one, once you've come to terms with the oven. I don't know why, but every cooker seems to be entirely different. If men had to do all the cooking, ovens would soon be perfect.

I've sorted out some of my best recipes for you. They've all been tried out at the Rovers and if I say so myself, they go down very well indeed.

STEAK AND KIDNEY PIE

Serves 4
1LB/450G STEWING STEAK
4OZ/110G LAMBS' KIDNEY
OIL OR DRIPPING
1 ONION
1OZ/30G PLAIN FLOUR
1 PINT/570ML BEEF STOCK (SEE PAGE 10)
SALT AND PEPPER
8OZ /225G SHORTCRUST PASTRY (SEE PAGE 10)

1. Trim any fat and cut the meat into bite-size chunks.
2. Skin, core and chop the kidneys.
3. Chop the onion and fry in a large saucepan in the oil or dripping for a few minutes.
4. Add the steak and kidney and brown all over.
5. Add the flour and stir for a minute or two.
6. Add the stock to the pan and simmer gently for about 2 hours, or until the meat is tender. Check the seasoning, adding salt and pepper if necessary.
7. Preheat the oven to 220°C/425°F/gas mark 7.
8. Put the meat in a pie dish. Cut a 1 inch strip of pastry and place round the dampened edge of the pie dish, wet lightly and lay the rolled-out pastry lid on top of it, pressing down the edges. Make a small hole in the centre to let out the steam.
9. Bake for 30-40 minutes until the pastry is golden brown.

Betty used to do everything by hand but these modern gadgets make everything a lot easier.

LANCASHIRE CHEESE AND ONION TARTS

Makes 18-24
10OZ/285G PUFF PASTRY
1OZ/30G BUTTER
1 ONION, FINELY CHOPPED
1OZ/30G FLOUR
1/2 PINT/290ML MILK
3 EGGS, SEPARATED
4OZ/110G LANCASHIRE CHEESE, GRATED
DRIED MIXED HERBS
SALT AND PEPPER

1. Preheat the oven to 220°C/425°F/gas mark 7.
2. Roll the pastry out thinly and line 18-24 tartlet tins.
3. Melt the butter in a pan, and gently fry the onion until it is soft.
4. Add the flour and stir well to avoid lumps. Cook for 1 minute.
5. Take the pan off the heat and slowly stir in the milk. Return to the heat and keep stirring as the sauce thickens.
6. Let the sauce cool a little and beat in the egg yolks.
7. Add the cheese, a pinch of herbs, salt and pepper and gently heat the mixture. Do not let it boil.
8. Beat the egg whites until stiff and carefully fold into the sauce.
9. Spoon the sauce into the tartlet cases and bake for 10-15 minutes until golden brown.

BEEF CASSEROLE AND DUMPLINGS

Serves 4
FOR THE CASSEROLE:
1LB/450G CHUCK STEAK
OIL FOR FRYING
1 LARGE ONION
2 CARROTS
1 TURNIP
HALF A SWEDE
1 TABLESPOON/30G PLAIN FLOUR
1 PINT/570ML HOT WATER
SALT AND PEPPER
BAY LEAF
1 TEASPOON/5ML DRIED THYME
FOR THE DUMPLINGS:
4OZ/110G SELF-RAISING FLOUR
2OZ/55G SHREDDED SUET
SALT AND PEPPER

1. Preheat the oven to 150°C/300°F/gas mark 2.
2. Cube the meat and brown quickly in the oil in a large frying pan.
3. Put the meat in a flame-proof casserole dish.
4. Fry the onions and root vegetables quickly and put in the casserole with the meat.
5. Stir the flour into the remaining oil in the pan, adding a little more oil if there isn't enough. Stir as the flour browns.
6. Gradually add the hot water and keep stirring. Season with salt, pepper, the bay leaf and herbs.
7. Pour the liquid over the meat and vegetables in the casserole.
8. Put the lid on the casserole and bake in the oven for 2 hours, until the meat is tender.
9. Meanwhile, make the dumplings: sift the flour into a basin and mix in the suet and salt and pepper.
10. Add enough cold water to make a smooth but not too sticky dough.
11. Divide into 12 small balls.
12. Take the casserole out of the oven and place the balls on top of the liquid.
13. Put back the lid and simmer on top of the cooker for 25 minutes.

MANCHESTER TART

Serves 4-6
8OZ/225G SHORTCRUST PASTRY (SEE PAGE 10)
2OZ/55G JAM
1 EGG
1/2 PINT/290ML MILK
SALT
NUTMEG
CASTER SUGAR

1. Preheat the oven to 220°C/425°F/gas mark 7.
2. Roll out the pastry and line a fairly shallow buttered 8-9 inch/20-22.5cm pie dish with it.
3. Spread the jam over the pastry.
4. Beat the egg into the milk and add a pinch of salt to taste.
5. Pour the mixture into the pie dish.
6. Grate a little nutmeg over the top.
7. Bake for 30 minutes until set.
8. Sprinkle with caster sugar, and serve hot or cold.

CHORLEY CAKES

Makes 4
1LB/450G SHORTCRUST PASTRY (SEE PAGE 10)
4OZ/110G CURRANTS
4OZ/110G CASTER SUGAR
4OZ/110G BUTTER
MILK

1. Preheat the oven to 180°C/350°F/gas mark 4.
2. Roll out the pastry until it is about 1/4 inch thick and cut into 4 rounds.
3. Put 1oz/30g of currants in the middle of each round, spreading them out a little bit but avoiding the edges.
4. Sprinkle 1oz/30g of sugar over each round and dot with 1oz/30g of butter.
5. Damp the edges of each circle and draw them into the centre, pressing together to seal.
6. Turn the cakes over and lightly roll them out, keeping the round shape, until the currants begin to show through.
7. Using a knife, score the tops with 3 parallel lines and brush with milk.
8. Bake for 25-30 minutes, or until lightly browned.

BETTY TURPIN

However awful life might be outside the Rovers, Betty's always waiting there with a plate of her hotpot – guaranteed to soothe the most troubled brow.

LEGENDARY THROUGHOUT WEATHERFIELD for her hotpot and pies, Betty has been pulling pints and serving snacks at The Rovers for over twenty years. Now a widow, Betty was married to a policeman, Cyril, and she still lives in the house they bought together, in nearby Hillside Crescent. A sweet and steady Weatherfield senior citizen, Betty nevertheless has an old skeleton in her cupboard. Years ago, she had an affair – and a son, Gordon, that husband Cyril never knew existed. Betty's sister Maggie brought up Gordon as her own, but mother and son have since been united again. Gordon lives down in London, and would like Betty to do the same. But old friends and older memories keep her in Weatherfield, and though Alec did once try and give her the push from behind the bar as a cost-cutting exercise, the regulars couldn't contemplate the thought of a Rovers Return minus Betty. When it comes to good traditional food there's not much that Betty doesn't know and if you follow her advice you won't go far wrong.

Victoria loves it when Betty makes her a special Victoria Sandwich.

50

VICTORIA SANDWICH

I always make one of these for Victoria when she comes to stay at the Rovers because the name makes her laugh.

4 oz/110g butter or margarine, at room temperature
4oz/110g caster sugar
2 large eggs
4oz/110g plain flour
1/2 teaspoon/2.5ml baking powder
jam
icing sugar

1. Preheat the oven to 170°C/325°F/gas mark 3.

2. Grease 2 x 7-inch/18cm sponge tins and line the bases with greaseproof paper.

3. Cream together the fat and sugar until they're soft and fluffy.

4. Beat the eggs together well and gradually add to the butter and sugar mixture just a little bit at a time. Beat well after each addition to prevent the mixture from curdling.

5. Sieve some of the flour and baking powder into the mixture, and gently fold in. Repeat until all the flour has been folded in.

6. Divide the mixture equally between the two prepared tins.

7. Bake in the centre of the oven for 25-30 minutes, or until the centres are springy to the touch.

8. Wait a minute and then turn them out on to a wire tray.

9. Let them cool, then sandwich them with jam and dust the top with icing sugar.

MANCHESTER PUDDING

Serves 4
1 pint/570ml milk
1oz/30g butter
4oz/110g white breadcrumbs
2oz/55g caster sugar
grated rind of 1 lemon
2 eggs
2oz/55g melted raspberry jam

1. Preheat the oven to 180°C/350°F/gas mark 4.

2. Bring the milk to the boil. Remove from the heat and stir in the butter, breadcrumbs, half the sugar and the grated lemon rind.

3. Leave for 10 minutes to let the breadcrumbs swell up.

4. Separate the egg yolks from the whites and beat them.

5. Add the yolks to the breadcrumb mixture and pour it all into a buttered 1 1/2 pint pie dish.

6. Warm the jam and lightly brush it over the surface of the mixture.

7. Beat the egg whites until they're stiff, beat in the rest of the sugar and spoon the meringue mixture over the pudding.

8. Bake for 30 minutes until light golden.

9. Serve cold.

BAKED CUSTARD TART

Serves 6
8oz/225g shortcrust pastry (see page 10)
1/2 pint/290ml milk
3 egg yolks
1 1/2oz/45g caster sugar
nutmeg

1. Preheat the oven to 200°C/400°F/gas mark 6.

2. Line an 8 inch/20cm pie dish with the pastry.

3. Heat the milk but don't let it boil.

4. Lightly beat the egg yolks with the sugar and then pour on the milk, beating all the time.

5. Pour the custard into the pie dish and grate a little nutmeg over the top.

6. Bake for 10 minutes. Turn down the oven to 180°C/350°F/gas mark 4 for another 30-35 minutes until the custard has set.

PHYLLIS

IT'S IMPORTANT TO LOOK AFTER YOURSELF when you get to my age, even when it seems too much trouble. Most of the dishes I do, I make last two or three meals. Just be sure to keep them in the fridge and to heat them properly and you'll be all right.

I must admit that making enough for two means that you can always offer a guest something to eat should anybody call, but nobody ever seems to bother these days. I keep asking Percy but he's a stubborn old fool. It'd make a lot of sense if we shared our expenses, but he won't have it. Anyway, here are some of my favourites for you to try. None of them cost much, so you don't have to worry.

SCOTCH BROTH

It's best to make this a day ahead. It will cool and the fat will rise to the top so that you can lift it off. It'll keep well in the fridge, so will do you for a few days. These amounts make three or four good bowls.

Serves 3-4
1LB/450G NECK OF LAMB
3 PINTS/1.75 LITRES WATER
2OZ/55G PEARL BARLEY
SALT AND PEPPER
1 ONION
1 CARROT
1 TURNIP
1 LEEK

1. Chop the lamb into chunks.
2. Put the lamb in a large pan with the water and bring to the boil.
3. Skim any scum that rises to the surface.
4. Add the rinsed barley, salt and pepper, cover and simmer for 1 hour.
5. Peel and chop the vegetables into small 1/4 inch/0.5cm dice. Add to the pot and simmer for another hour.
6. Remove the lamb from the pan and separate the meat from the bones and fat. Return the meat to the pan.
7. Let the soup go cold and next day lift off any fat that's risen to the top.
8. Reheat before serving.

Left: Phyllis dreams of the day that Percy will arrive as her knight in shining armour!

STUFFED BREAST OF LAMB

When you're on a pension it's not easy to buy any meat, let alone expensive stuff like steak. Fortunately cheap cuts of meat are the best ones for taste as long as you cook them slowly. Breast of lamb is cheap but it needs proper cooking to give its best. Get the butcher to bone it for you and hang on to the bones to roast with the breast for a bit and then use them for a good thick gravy. You can always buy one ready stuffed and that's a good buy. Whichever way you do it, cook it long and slow. In fact, it's a good dish to cook very slowly all day so you've got a meal to come home to if you're going out. You can make your own stuffing or you can use a packet of thyme and parsley stuffing.

Serves 2
1 BREAST OF LAMB, ABOUT 2LB/900G BONED
FOR THE STUFFING:
1 TABLESPOON/15ML FINELY CHOPPED ONION
1OZ/30G MARGARINE
2-3 TABLESPOONS/30-45ML FRESH WHITE BREADCRUMBS
1 EGG
1 TEASPOON/5ML DRIED THYME
GRATED RIND OF 1 LEMON
SALT AND PEPPER

1. Preheat the oven to 180°C/350°F/gas mark 4.
2. Soften the onion in the melted margarine.
3. Stir in the crumbs.
4. Add the beaten egg to the rest of the ingredients.
5. Spread the mixture over the breast and roll it up from thick to flap end, tucking in the flap end.
6. Tie the lamb with 2 or 3 lengths of string, not too tightly.
7. Put the meat in an oiled tin and cover with a foil lid. Roast for 2 hours. Remove the foil for the last half hour, and baste with the juices in the tin.

PHYLLIS PEARCE

WITH HER EXTRAVAGANTLY TINTED HAIR and peppery passion for fellow pensioner Percy Sugden, Phyllis is a senior citizen with spirit. She lives in a bungalow in nearby Gorton Close – and after first meeting Percy back in 1985, she's been trying to get him to move in with her ever since.

Though she's been retired for a good few years now, Phyllis keeps herself active and supplements her pension by cleaning for Des Barnes and Alf and Audrey Roberts. She has a particular soft spot for Des, and was greatly upset when wife Steph walked out on him. Des has very much become the son that Phyllis never had. She's also a dab hand at serving in Jim's Café. When Gail or Alma are pushed for staff, they usually ask Phyllis to come in and cover, though it's not always been sweetness and light between them. Alma once gave her the sack for rowing with Percy over the counter.

Sadly, Phyllis's husband Frank and daughter Margaret are both now dead – but she does have a grandson, Craig, who lives out in Australia.

Many men would appreciate a woman as faithful as Phyllis – but not Percy.

BAKED PORK CHOP WITH PICKLE

Serves 1
1OZ/30G BUTTER
A LITTLE OIL
1 SLICE OF ONION CHOPPED FINE
1 PORK CHOP
1 TABLESPOON/15ML PICCALILLI
PINCH OF DRIED MARJORAM
SALT AND PEPPER

1. Preheat the oven to 180°C/350°F/gas mark 4.
2. Melt the butter with a little oil and brown the chop on both sides. Remove from the pan.
3. Cut a square of foil large enough to wrap the chop in and put the chop in the middle of the foil.
4. Add a little more butter or oil to the pan if necessary, and fry the onion gently until it's soft.
5. Put the onion and piccalilli on top of the chop and sprinkle with marjoram, salt and pepper.
6. Loosely wrap the chop in the foil and fold the edges over to seal the parcel.
7. Bake for 40 minutes.
8. Serve with chips and a green vegetable.

BACON AND EGG PIE

Serves 4
8OZ/225G SHORTCRUST PASTRY (SEE PAGE 10)
4OZ/110G BACON
3 EGGS
A LITTLE MILK
SALT AND PEPPER

1. Preheat the oven to 190°C/375°/gas mark 5.
2. Line an 8 inch/20cm pie dish with half the pastry.
3. Cut the rind off the bacon and chop finely.
4. Beat the eggs with a little milk and add salt and pepper.
5. Spread the chopped bacon over the pastry and pour the egg mixture over it.
6. Roll out the rest of the pastry and cover the pie.
7. Seal the edges of the pastry and make a hole in the centre of the top to let out steam. Brush with a little milk.
8. Bake for 25 minutes and then turn the oven down to 170°C/325°F/gas mark 3 for a further 25 minutes
9. Serve hot or cold

GLAZED BACON JOINT

Serves 3-4
1 BACON JOINT APPROXIMATELY 11/2LB/675G
1 TABLESPOON/15ML MADE MUSTARD
2 TABLESPOONS/30ML BROWN SUGAR

1. Put the joint in a saucepan of cold water. Bring to the boil and then throw away the water. This gets rid of the salt.
2. Start again and simmer the bacon for 30 minutes.
3. Preheat the oven to 190°C/375°F/gas mark 5.
4. Remove the bacon from the water and strip off any rind.
5. Spread the mustard over the bacon and sprinkle the sugar over it.
6. Bake for 20 minutes, basting it frequently.

RICE PUDDING

Serves 4
2OZ/55G SHORT-GRAIN PUDDING RICE, WASHED
1/2OZ/15G BUTTER, PLUS EXTRA TO GREASE PIE DISH
11/2OZ/45G SUGAR
1 PINT/570ML MILK
GRATED NUTMEG

1. Preheat the oven to 150°C/300°F/gas mark 2.
2. Put the rice into a buttered pie dish with the sugar.
3. Stir in the milk, sprinkle with nutmeg and dot with butter.
4. Bake for 3 hours. Stir in the skin at least once during the baking.

There's nothing better than home-made rice pudding.

DEIRDRE AND TRACY'S BONFIRE NIGHT SPREAD

Deirdre and Tracy launch a night of bonfire fun.

I'VE ALWAYS LOVED BUMMY PLOT. I think everybody does. We all claim it's for the kids but really it's for us as well. Now Tracy's older she doesn't get quite as excited as she used to, but that just means she doesn't spend weeks rushing round like a lunatic. When I was a kid we used to make rival bonfires in every street and steal each other's wood. These days it's a lot more sedate but it's still fun. The food is always one of the best things.

Pea soup isn't just for Bonfire Plot. It's a very good winter warmer whenever the weather is bad.

PEA SOUP

Serves 6
BACON SHANK
8OZ/225G SPLIT PEAS
8OZ/225G CARROTS, CHOPPED
4OZ/110G SWEDE, CHOPPED
I LARGE ONION, CHOPPED
GOOD PINCH OF MIXED HERBS

1. Bring the bacon shank to the boil in 3 pints/1.75 litres of water. Spoon off the scum as it rises to the top.
2. Add the split peas, the chopped vegetables and a good pinch of mixed herbs.
3. Simmer for 1½ hours stirring occasionally.
4. Take the bacon shank out of the pan and remove the meat from the bone. Return the meat to the pan.
5. Taste the soup and add seasoning if required.

BLACK PEAS

Serves 6-8
8OZ/225G BLACK PEAS
I LARGE ONION
3 PINTS/1.75 LITRES WATER
VINEGAR
SALT AND PEPPER

1. Soak the peas overnight. Drain.
2. Chop the onion and add to the peas. Cover with the water and simmer for about an hour, or until cooked. Top up with water if it gets too thick.
3. Add seasoning to taste and serve with vinegar.

Note: If you have trouble buying black peas you can usually find them in pet shops.

BAKED POTATOES

Choose good-sized potatoes. King Edward's is a good variety.

I POTATO PER PERSON
BUTTER
SALT AND PEPPER

1. Preheat the oven to 200°C/400°F/gas mark 6.
2. Scrub the potatoes and dry them.
3. Prick all over with a fork.
4. Bake for 45-60 minutes. Insert a skewer to make sure they're done.
5. Cut the potatoes in half and serve with a blob of butter, salt and pepper.

Note: If you're cooking them in the bonfire, wrap each potato in a double layer of foil and bury in the embers.

PARKIN

8OZ/225G MEDIUM OATMEAL
4OZ/110G PLAIN FLOUR
2 TEASPOONS/10ML GROUND GINGER
4OZ/110G MARGARINE
6OZ/170G SUGAR
8OZ/225G TREACLE
1/2 TEASPOON/2.5ML BICARBONATE OF SODA MIXED WITH A
LITTLE MILK
I EGG

1. Preheat the oven to 150°C/300°F/gas mark 2.
2. Mix together the oatmeal, flour and ground ginger.
3. Melt the margarine, sugar and treacle in a saucepan and add to the dry ingredients.
4. Add the egg, bicarbonate of soda and milk to the mixture.
5. Blend thoroughly.
6. Spoon the mixture into a well-greased baking tin about 8 inches/20cm square and bake for 90 minutes or until the centre feels springy to the touch.
7. Cut into squares when cold.

TREACLE TOFFEE

ILB/450G DEMERARA SUGAR
8OZ/225G BLACK TREACLE
4OZ/110G BUTTER
I TABLESPOON/15ML MALT VINEGAR
I TABLESPOON/15ML WATER

1. Put the sugar, black treacle, butter, vinegar and water into a pan.
2. Stir over a low heat until the sugar is dissolved.
3. Bring to the boil and boil rapidly without stirring for 10-15 minutes.
4. If you've got a sugar thermometer, the temperature should reach 140°C/280°F. If you haven't got a thermometer, drop a little toffee into a saucer of cold water. If it hardens, the toffee is ready.
5. Pour the toffee into a greased tin and just before it sets mark into squares.

DEIRDRE AND TRACY BARLOW

Nobody's ever too old to enjoy Bonfire Plot. Deirdre and Tracy love it!

RAY LANGTON, father of Tracy, was the great love of Deirdre's life but their marriage foundered after just three years. Her life since then has been a series of dramatic highs and lows: another marriage and another divorce; an extra-marital affair with Mike Baldwin; sexual assault; depression verging on suicide; the struggle to raise a daughter single-handed and hold down a responsible position as a councillor, not to mention coping with an assortment of very different – if equally unreliable – men.

Tracy herself was feared dead when a lorry careered into the front of the Rovers Return, leaving the spot where her pram was parked a mass of rubble. She lived to tell the tale and has grown up a typical moody teenager, occasionally getting into trouble for playing truant to spend time in the amusement arcade. Deirdre's common sense and fairness as a mother mean Tracy can just about forgive her her penchant for curly perms, penny-round collars and unsuitable men. These days, Deidre is cynical about romantic involvement, not wanting to get her fingers burnt again. Nevertheless, with the loss of her place on the Council and the prospect of Tracy leaving the nest, Deirdre sometimes gets frustrated with her job at the Corner Shop and occasionally can't stop herself doing something different.

MIKE BALDWIN

WITH LIVING IN LANCASHIRE for so long I've got used to the local food and I must admit I enjoy it. But there are times when I want a little taste of London, so I get in the kitchen and make some of the dishes I've loved all my life.

Alma's not very keen on my eels and mash but she likes my bubble and squeak and just loves my spotted dick. Maybe I'll persuade her to start selling them in the café and then I won't have to make them myself.

BUBBLE AND SQUEAK

Traditionally this is made with leftovers but if you haven't got any it's so good it's worth starting from scratch. Serve it for breakfast with a couple of rashers of bacon and a fried egg.

Serves 2
1LB/450G BOILED POTATOES
2OZ/55G BUTTER
8OZ/225G COOKED CABBAGE OR SPROUTS
SALT AND PEPPER
DRIPPING
FLOUR

1. Mash the potatoes with the butter and add the cabbage or sprouts.
2. Mix them together and season with salt and pepper.
3. Melt some dripping in the frying pan.
4. Shape the bubble and squeak into flat round shapes.
5. Dust with a little flour and fry on both sides until brown.
6. Alternatively make one large cake and cut portions from it after you've cooked it.

Mike hasn't managed to persuade Alma to start selling jellied eels yet, but there's still time.

EELS AND MASH

When I was a nipper there were lots of eel and pie shops but there aren't many left now. There's certainly none in Weatherfield so here's how to make the classic eels and mash.

Serves 2
1LB/450G EELS
LEMON JUICE
1OZ/30G FLOUR
2OZ/55G BUTTER
SALT AND PEPPER
PARSLEY
1LB/450G POTATOES

1. Buy the eels skinned and chopped.
2. Cover with salted water in a pan and add a little lemon juice.
3. Cover the pan and simmer gently for about 30-40 minutes until tender.
4. Reserve $1/2$ pint/290ml of the liquid and put the eel pieces on a plate in a low oven to keep warm.
5. Make a sauce with the flour, half the butter, and cooking liquid (see Betty's Basics, page 11).
6. Add finely chopped parsley to the sauce. Taste and season with salt and pepper.
7. Boil and mash the potatoes with the remaining butter.
8. Divide the eels between 2 soup bowls. Pour over a liitle sauce and put a serving of mashed potato on the side of each one.

Mike has introduced Alma to lots of delights, including his bubble and squeak.

WHITEBAIT

Serves 4
FLOUR
SALT AND PEPPER
1LB/450G WHITEBAIT
OIL FOR DEEP-FRYING

1. Get a large paper bag and put the flour and some salt and pepper in it. Give it a good shake.
2. Put the whitebait in the bag and shake it so as to coat the fish with the seasoned flour.
3. Fry them a few at a time in the oil in a chip pan for no more than 2 minutes. Don't put them all in at once or they'll just stick together.
4. Serve with wedges of lemon.

SPOTTED DICK

My old mum used to do this for us. This isn't as good as she used to make but it's not bad. Serve with lots of custard and a spoonful of jam.

Serves 4
8OZ/225G PLAIN FLOUR
4OZ/110G SHREDDED SUET
3OZ/85G CASTER SUGAR
1/2OZ/15G BAKING POWDER
1/4 PINT/150ML MILK
4OZ/110G RAISINS OR CURRANTS

1. Mix together all the dry ingredients except for the raisins.
2. Add the milk and mix to a stiff consistency.
3. Roll out the pastry into a rectangular shape about 12 inches/30cm long and 1/2 inch/1cm thick.
4. Spread the raisins over the pastry, pressing them in and leaving a 1/2 inch margin all the way round.
5. Moisten the edges and roll up from one of the long edges.
6. Seal the edge and roll in a floured pudding cloth.
7. Boil or steam for 1 1/2 hours.

MIKE BALDWIN

ENTREPRENEUR EXTRAORDINAIRE, Mike has always had an eye for a business opportunity, investing in everything from motor spares to real estate over the years. It was business that first brought the chirpy Londoner to Weatherfield back in 1976, when he opened up a factory making denim outfits – and ended up employing half the women from Coronation Street at his machines.

A man who likes his cigars and whiskies large, his women glamorous and his cars flash and speedy, Mike has never been one for the quiet life. He made an arch enemy out of Ken Barlow by first conducting a steamy and passionate affair with Ken's then wife, Deirdre, and then by marrying and splitting up with his daughter Susan. He courted Alma Sedgewick and then dumped her for a wealthy widowed businesswoman, Jackie Ingram. They made it to the altar, but the marriage lasted all of a week. Just to add insult to previous injury, Mike then stole Alma back from her new beau, Ken Barlow, and eventually convinced her to tie the knot with him. He has a young son by local florist Maggie Redman, but she's sworn him to secrecy over the whole affair.

Mike's always ready to celebrate a stroke of luck, especially his own.

IVY'S FISH DISHES

AS A CATHOLIC I know you don't have to eat fish on Fridays any more but I always feel guilty eating meat, so usually me and Don just stick to fish. Not that it's a hardship as both of us love it. Sometimes we just go to the chippy, but as often as not we take a little bit of trouble and do something a bit special.

It helps working at Bettabuys because the fish counter is very good and I can bring stuff home with me. All of these recipes are easy and I've included potted shrimps specially because they're Don's favourite.

If you're feeling a bit flush then try the salmon steaks, but you'll find the cheesey fish cakes very tasty, and very cheap to make.

FISH TARTS

Makes 6
8OZ/225G SHORTCRUST PASTRY (SEE PAGE 10)
8OZ/225G COD OR OTHER WHITE FISH
MILK
3OZ/85G BUTTER
1¹/₂OZ/45G PLAIN FLOUR
I SMALL ONION
2OZ/55G MUSHROOMS
2OZ/55G LANCASHIRE CHEESE

1. Preheat the oven to 190°C/375°F/gas mark 5.
2. Roll out the pastry and line 6 small tart tins with it.
3. Bake blind (line the pastry case with foil and fill with dried beans) for 10 minutes, remove the foil and beans and cook for a further 5 minutes or until golden brown.
4. Meanwhile, cover the cod with milk and poach gently till cooked.
5. Following Betty's recipe on page 11, make a white sauce, using 1 pint/570ml of the poaching liquid in place of the milk and stock, 2oz/55g of the butter and all the flour.
6. Sauté the onions in half the remaining butter until soft. Add to the white sauce.
7. Wipe or peel the mushrooms, slice and sauté gently in the remaining butter until soft and the liquid has evaporated. Add to the white sauce.
8. Fold in the flaked fish and divide between the tarts. Sprinkle with the grated cheese.
9. Grill to brown the tops and serve.

It doesn't matter to Ivy if they're big or little – she can still cook them!

FISH PLATE PIE

Serves 4
1LB/450G WHITING OR COD FILLET
5 TABLESPOONS/75ML WATER
I SMALL ONION
2OZ/55G MUSHROOMS
SALT AND PEPPER
8OZ/225G SHORTCRUST PASTRY (SEE PAGE 10)
2 EGGS
PARSLEY

1. Preheat the oven to 190°C/375°F/gas mark 5.
2. Try to take as many bones out of the fish as you can and discard any skin.
3. Put the fish, water, finely chopped onion, washed and sliced mushrooms and a little seasoning into a pan and simmer for 5-10 minutes.
4. Roll out the pastry and line a pie dish with half the pastry.
5. Let the fish mixture cool down a bit and add the beaten eggs and chopped parsley. Save a little egg for glazing the pastry.
6. Spread the mixture on the pie dish and cover with the other half of the pastry. Brush with a little beaten egg and bake for 25-30 minutes or until golden brown.

SALMON STEAKS

Wrap 1 salmon steak per person in buttered foil with a slice of lemon, salt and pepper, and bake at 190°C/375°F/gas mark 5 for 20 minutes.

DON AND IVY BRENNAN

B Y ANYBODY'S STANDARDS Don and Ivy have had tragic lives. She lost her first husband, Bert, and her son, Brian. He lost his first wife, Pat, and has little contact with his children. To add to their tragedy Don had a serious car accident as a result of his affair with barmaid Julie Dewhurst and had to have his foot amputated.

Ivy now works at Bettabuys with Vera but in the past she spent many years working for Mike Baldwin, where her strict standards of behaviour often led to conflict with him. These days she is no longer a shop steward and has enough on her plate with Don without looking for trouble at Bettabuys.

Ivy is not the most popular person with her neighbours in The Street because of her holier than thou attitude to life but she gets on well with her best friend Vera. They live next door to each other and their lives are constantly intertwined. Her daughter-in-law Gail and husband Martin find her a bit of a strain, especially when she interferes in her grandson Nicky's life, but they put up with her.

In general there's not a lot in life that Ivy approves of and Don is pretty long-suffering. But one thing they do agree on is food. Perhaps as well.

Don, Ivy and Alf discussing the relative merits of offal and fish!

CHEESEY FISH CAKES

Serves 2
1LB/450G POTATOES
MILK
1/2 BUNCH SPRING ONIONS
PARSLEY
1 TIN SARDINES
4OZ/110G LANCASHIRE CHEESE, GRATED
SALT AND PEPPER
FLOUR
OIL AND BUTTER

1. Peel the potatoes, boil until cooked, and mash with a very little milk.
2. Chop the spring onions and parsley very finely.
3. Mash the sardines with the potatoes, parsley, spring onions and cheese. Season with salt and pepper.
4. Divide the mixture into four and make into rounds. Dust with flour.
5. Fry in equal quantities of oil and butter until crisp on both sides.
6. Serve with chips and tomato sauce.

Fish cakes are very cheap to make and Ivy has been glad of them when times have been hard. Adding a bit of cheese makes them just that little bit special.

POTTED SHRIMPS

Serves 4
6OZ/170G UNSALTED BUTTER
1/4 TEASPOON MACE
1/4 TEASPOON GROUND NUTMEG
PINCH OF CAYENNE PEPPER
8OZ/225G COOKED AND PEELED SHRIMPS
SALT
LEMON
TOAST

1. Melt the butter and add the spices. Simmer very gently to develop the flavour.
2. Add the shrimps and simmer gently for 20 minutes. Keep stirring them to avoid browning.
3. Pack into small pots and top up with clarified butter to cover.
4. Keep in the fridge and once you've opened them eat within 48 hours.
5. Serve with toast, lemon, salt and pepper.

SMOKED FINNAN HADDOCK WITH EGG SAUCE

Serves 2-3
1LB/450G OF SMOKED HADDOCK
1/2 PINT/290ML MILK
1 BAY LEAF
PEPPER
1OZ/30G BUTTER
3/4OZ/20G PLAIN FLOUR
2 HARD-BOILED EGGS
PARSLEY

1. Simmer the haddock, skin side down, in the milk with the bay leaf and pepper for 10 minutes.
2. Remove the bay leaf and use 1/2 pint/290ml of the cooking liquid, the butter and flour to make a white sauce, following Betty's instructions on page 11.
3. Chop the eggs and add to the sauce with the chopped parsley.
4. Serve the fish with the sauce and boiled potatoes.

CHRISTMAS WITH GAIL AND MARTIN

IF YOUR HOUSE IS ANYTHING LIKE OURS, having to sort out which of the relatives are coming and who hates who and who doesn't causes so much trouble I feel like locking the front door and not bothering with any of it, but in the end I always do.

I claim it's all for the kids but it isn't really. I always live in hope that everything's going to be wonderful and everybody's going to get on and there's going to be no rows, but usually I consider myself lucky if there's been no fighting. You'd think that Audrey and Ivy could call a truce for one day a year, but I suppose they've had so much practice at smiling at each other and trading insults at the same time that it just comes naturally.

But even if the relatives are driving you daft it's important to make the cooking as stress free as possible. That means planning ahead, having a timetable and doing your best to keep to it.

TURKEY DINNER TIMETABLE

Unless you really enjoy flying around like a lunatic, then make things like mince pies before the day itself. Better still, buy them. You should have made your Christmas pudding ages before, but if you forgot you can buy good ones in the shops, so don't panic. The main meal is the thing to concentrate on.

Serves 12-14
12-14LB/6KG TURKEY
8OZ/225G STREAKY BACON
6OZ/170G BUTTER
FOR THE STUFFING:
1½LB/675G WHITE BREADCRUMBS
LARGE BUNCH OF PARSLEY
2 TABLESPOONS/30ML DRIED THYME
SALT AND PEPPER
2 LEMONS
4OZ/110G BUTTER
4 EGGS

1. Order a fresh turkey well before Christmas. When you get it home remove the giblets. Remember to have the turkey at room temperature before putting it in the oven.
2. On Christmas Eve make the stock for gravy with the giblets. (See page 37 for making giblet stock.)
3. On the morning itself, get up good and early. If you aim to eat at about 3 pm, everybody can have a drink in the Rovers before you get started.

It isn't easy for Gail and Martin to find a moment to themselves at Christmas.

4. Aim at getting the bird in the oven for 10 am.
5. Make the stuffing first. Mix together the breadcrumbs, chopped parsley, thyme, salt and pepper. Squeeze the juice out of the lemons and grate the rind. Add to the stuffing.
6. Melt the 4oz/110g of butter and add to the stuffing along with the beaten eggs.
7. Loosen the skin round the neck end with your fingers and push a little of the stuffing in to make a nice rounded shape, but remember not to make it too tight as it'll expand during cooking.
8. Put the rest of the stuffing into the body.
9. Put the oven on to 220°C/425°F/gas mark 7.
10. Get your turkey foil and line your baking tray with two long sheets, each going in opposite directions so that it will be easier to parcel up the turkey.
11. Put the turkey breast side up in the tray and rub the remaining 6oz/170g of butter all over the body. Season with salt and pepper and overlap the bacon on the breast.
12. Fold over the foil to make an airtight but loose parcel.
13. Put the bird in the oven on a low shelf and cook for 45 minutes, then turn it down to 170°C/325°F/gas mark 3 for 3 hours. Then remove the foil on top of the bird and the bacon. Turn the oven up to 200°C/400°F/gas mark 6 for 30 minutes to brown it. Keep basting it during this last bit.
14. Ten minutes before opening up the foil on the turkey, boil some potatoes and parsnips for 10 minutes and stick them round the bird to roast. If there isn't enough room, spoon some fat from around the turkey into another baking tray and roast them separately in the oven.
15. Test to see if the turkey is cooked by piercing the thickest part of the leg with a skewer. If the juices run clear, it is cooked. Remove from the oven and leave to rest in a warm place for 20-30 minutes.

Producing Christmas Dinner and all the trimmings is a big job, even for Gail.

BREAD SAUCE

3OZ/85G BREAD
2OZ/55G BUTTER
³/4 PINT/425ML MILK
I LARGE ONION STUCK WITH A FEW CLOVES
SALT AND PEPPER

I. Tear the bread into large bits. Put all the ingredients into a pan.

2. Put the pan on a low heat and up break the bread as the milk heats.

3. When it comes to the boil, whisk the bread into the milk and simmer for 5 minutes, stirring constantly.

4. Put the lid on the pan, take it off the heat and let it stand for 45 minutes.

5. Discard the onion.

6. When you need it, reheat the sauce gently, adding a little milk if it's too thick.

GAIL AND MARTIN PLATT

At Christmas Gail and Martin like to deck the boughs with sprigs of holly – but hopefully no Ivy.

GAIL TILSEY caused a storm by taking Martin Platt as her toyboy in 1989. Now they are happily married with a baby son, David, and live at No. 8. Gail has two other children, Nicky and Sarah Louise, from her previous marriage to Brian Tilsey.

Gail's marriage to Brian was often stormy. They married at 21 and she had Nicky when she was 22. They both had affairs and she slept with his cousin Ian Latimer. Her admission that she was pregnant and she didn't know who the father was caused Brian to leave her. Ian took a blood test that proved he wasn't Sarah Louise's father but this didn't help.

Brian's kidnapping of Nicky made him realize he needed Gail and they all needed each other. The Tilseys remarried in 1988, just after their divorce was finalized. Gail knew it was a mistake to marry Brian again and within a year told him she wanted another divorce. That night he was murdered outside a night club.

Gail is now Alma's partner in the café and she met Martin Platt while he was working there.

Martin has defied all expectations by proving to be a supportive husband and father – never ashamed to iron a shirt or change a dirty nappy – while still remaining one of the lads. During a spell as a hospital porter he saved the life of an elderly woman and realized that his ambitions extended beyond pushing trolleys. He gained a place on the nursing course at Weatherfield General, which opened up a whole new social life for him. Gail initially resented this but has since made friends with some of his colleagues. Martin often struggles with the academic course work, but no one doubts he'll make a good nurse in the end.

MARTIN'S BOXING DAY BREAKFAST

AFTER ALL THE HARD WORK Gail's put in I like to give her a treat on Boxing Day. She gets a cup of tea in bed and I manage to waylay the kids downstairs, where they can argue and hit each other with their new toys while I make Gail and me a super-duper special breakfast.

You have to do your share sometime, so it might as well be breakfast as at least it gives you the rest of the day to recover. But to be honest, I like cooking breakfast. I had plenty of practice when I was working in the café and it's not too difficult as long as you don't start cooking till you've got everything ready. Otherwise everything happens too fast and you're trying to juggle three things at once and you lose your temper and it all ends in tears. But not the Martin Platt way!

Try to avoid frying everything. That's the medical training coming out in me. It's also a lot easier to grill, and most people will have a big enough grill pan for several people but probably won't have big enough frying pans. So it makes sense even if you're not bothered about your health.

As it's Christmas you can have a once-a-year treat with a couple of fried items, but if you regularly have fried eggs and bacon and whatever else you like, all swimming in grease, then you won't be seeing that many more Christmases. On that happy little note, let's get stuck in.

This is for two people. If you've got more just double or treble up. If your grill pan isn't big enough for everybody, then do the meats first and then put them on a plate and stick it in a very low oven to keep warm. If you've got kids, feed them first and then get rid of them, as this is your treat.

Whatever the occasion, the kids are more than happy to join in.

Serves 2
TEA
4 RASHERS BACON
2 SAUSAGES
2 TOMATOES
SALT AND PEPPER
8 BUTTON MUSHROOMS
BUTTER OR OLIVE OIL
1 BLACK PUDDING
2 LEFTOVER BOILED POTATOES
BREAD FOR TOAST
2 EGGS
1 SLICE BREAD FOR FRIED BREAD
MARMALADE

1. Set the table ready to eat. If you start trying to do this once you're cooking you'll end up with a disaster.
2. Fill the kettle and get the teapot ready for making tea.
3. If you don't like the rind, cut it off the bacon. If you like it, snip it through every so often to stop the bacon curling up.
4. Turn the grill on to let it get hot.
5. Put the bacon on the grill pan with the sausages. Prick the sausages with a fork.
6. Wash the tomatoes and slice in 2. Sprinkle a little salt and pepper on them. Put them on the grill pan.
7. Wipe the mushrooms and put them in a small pan with salt and pepper and a little butter or oil. Olive oil's the best. Cover tightly and put on very low heat on top of the cooker.

8. Peel and slice the black pudding lengthways in 2 and put on the grill pan.
9. Slice the potatoes.
10. Have the frying pan ready with a little oil in it.
11. Brush the sausages and tomatoes with a little oil and put under the hot grill.
12. Put 2 plates in low oven to warm.
13. Put the potatoes to fry in the hot frying pan. Keep moving them round. Shake the mushroom pan.
14. Turn the potatoes over when they've browned on one side.
15. Turn the sausage and bacon and pudding over.
16. Boil the kettle, put tea in the pot and fill.
17. If you use a toaster, start feeding it with slices of bread. If not wait until the grill is clear or pretend it's fashionable to serve toast after breakfast.
18. Take out the hot plates and put the potatoes on them.
19. Break 2 eggs gently into the frying pan. Slice the bread for the fried bread into 2 triangles and put in the pan too.
20. Put the mushrooms on the plates.
21. Divide everything on the grill pan between the plates. Turn over the bread in the frying pan.
22. By this time the eggs will be cooked. Put them on the plates.
23. Shout to your other half, add the fried bread to the plates and serve breakfast.
24. Try and act relaxed, as though it's all very easy and you can't see what all the big deal is about. Gracefully accept all compliments and thanks.

After one of Martin's special breakfasts, it's a good idea to get out for a bit of fresh air.

73

KEN BARLOW'S WINE TIPS

'VE ALWAYS BEEN INTERESTED in the exciting things in life, ever since I was a student. In those days wine was something strange and foreign that ordinary people didn't drink. It was thought a bit snobbish to enjoy a glass of red with your evening meal. I'm glad to say that those days are long gone and people are drinking more and more wine every year.

Just because you enjoy wine doesn't mean you can't continue to enjoy beer. They're just different drinks. I do think, however, that some people are still a bit frightened of buying wine in case they buy the wrong thing and look ridiculous. Well that's really silly, because the right wine is simply the one that you enjoy drinking.

Years ago people used to give you strict rules about drinking wine. Which wine to drink with particular kinds of food and which wine to drink at particular times of day. That's all nonsense.

If you enjoy a particular wine you can drink it with any food you like and when you like, and don't let anybody tell you any different, because they'd be wrong.

Red or White? Sweet or Dry?

You can't go far wrong if you drink red with beef and lamb and white with pork, chicken and fish. But as always, don't follow this rule if you don't enjoy it. If you want to drink white wine with beef or red wine with fish go ahead and do it. I often do if I'm in the mood.

Most people start off appreciating sweet wine and move on to dry wine after they've got the taste for it. Sweet wines are generally drunk with desserts.

Where to Buy

Not many people know very much about wine, so if you find a shop with somebody who does, buy your wine there and stick to them. Otherwise you're better off shopping in the supermarkets. They have a huge range and their prices are very reasonable. Remember that not all cheap wines taste cheap.

Some supermarkets have little labels that give you a bit of information about the wine and this can be very useful. All of them have some system of labelling that tells you how sweet or dry the wine is, which is usually all you need to know to be able to judge whether a wine fits into your general taste range. The price is the other criterion!

I have some friends who buy all their wines on the basis of how pretty the label is. At least it means they get to drink lots of varieties, but it's no real test of how good the wine itself is. Making good wine and designing a good label are two completely different skills.

What to Buy

Here are a few wines that I learnt about at my Wine Appreciation classes. You can get all of them at supermarkets and they're all at the cheaper end of the market.

Sparkling Wines

Champagne is far too expensive for most of us, but sparkling wine is still a little bit special. Try a bottle of *Montana Lindauer,* from New Zealand. Good for a very special occasion or just to drink before a meal.

It didn't take Wine Appreciation evening classes to awaken Ken's interest in the grape but it certainly enhanced his knowledge to the point where he has no qualms about advising other people.

Although he shared many a glass of wine with Alma, Ken was eventually beaten to the altar by his rival, Mike Baldwin.

Red Wines

For a full-bodied red wine try a *Buzet Domaine de la Croix, 1988* from France. The English have always been keen on claret and most of the supermarkets have good cheap ones that are simply labelled with their own brand name. Marketed under its own name is a *Bergerac rouge* from *Cave de Sigoules*, France. A lovely, rich wine.

For a more full, spicy wine try a *Penfolds Bin 2 Shiraz 1989* from Australia.

Spanish reds are improving all the time. For an excellent oaky, blackcurranty wine try a *Don Darias red, Bodegas Vitorianas*. Very inexpensive for what it offers. Everybody I've given this to has loved it.

White Wines

A lot of people drink Chardonnay because it's the only white wine whose name they can remember. For a good one try a *Villard Chardonnay 1990* from Chile. It was always Alma's favourite.

As an alternative to Chardonnay try a *Saumur blanc*, for example *Caves des Vignerons de Saumur 1989* from France. It's a very good, fresh wine.

Rosé Wines

If you like drinking rosé wines for their pretty colour, then try white *Zinfandel* from California. It's coral pink with a grapefruity flavour.

Dessert Wines

If you've never had dessert wine, then try *Moscatel de Valencia* from Spain. It's wonderful with pudding.

All of these wines are tremendous value, so give them a try, or select something else that takes your fancy. That's what's so good about drinking wine. There's such a huge range available, you could drink a different variety every day for the rest of your life and never repeat the experience. That's what I call exciting!

KEN BARLOW

KEN BARLOW APPEARED in the very first episode of Coronation Street. In many ways he has had a tragic life but he hasn't allowed his misfortune to get the better of him. He has a degree in Modern English and has spent most of his adult years teaching, apart from a spell in the newspaper business running *The Recorder*.

His marriage to Deirdre fell apart because of his affair with Wendy Crozier, although Ken blamed Deirdre's Council work and her affair with Mike Baldwin. He had to sell *The Recorder* after the affair with Wendy Crozier as he had to give the family home to Deirdre.

After a failed suicide attempt Ken has resigned himself to the fact that Deirdre will not have him back. He does his best to do the right thing for Tracy but he has trouble accepting that she's growing up.

He had an affair with Alma Sedgewick after she had been dumped by his arch rival Mike Baldwin, but when Mike came back Alma chose him in preference to Ken.

These days he's back teaching English at the school where he was once Deputy Headmaster and he lives in a flat over the corner shop.

Over the years his hatred for Mike Baldwin has grown and his relationship with Mike is probably more influential on his life than any other factor.

Ken Barlow can teach you anything – including the best wines to drink.

PARTY BUFFET BY BETTY, GAIL AND ALMA

CORONATION STREET KNOWS how to throw a good party, whatever the occasion. Usually it's Betty and the girls from the café who do the honours, though sometimes Percy's catering experience is called upon. Des's surprise birthday party was just such an occasion and the whole street rallied round to help out.

It's as well to farm out the jobs to different people if you can. If you can't, then try and do as much as possible in advance and get a bit of help on the day.

Together these dishes will happily feed twenty people. If there are going to be more than that make additional main dishes as long as you've got help. If you haven't, just double up the quantities.

You can do most of the cold dishes well ahead, so with a bit of luck you might get a chance to have a drink yourself before the festivities begin.

The one point to remember is that once the party starts there's nothing you can do about anything, so just enjoy it. Worrying whether everything's all right won't change a thing.

CHICKEN WINGS WITH HOT TOMATO SAUCE

Serves 20 as part of a buffet
1 ONION
1 LARGE TIN OF TOMATOES
1/2 TEASPOON/2.5ML DRIED THYME
SALT AND PEPPER
20 CHICKEN WINGS
FRESH PARSLEY

1. Preheat the oven to 200°C/400°F/gas mark 6.
2. Gently fry the onion until soft.
3. Add the tomatoes and thyme.
4. Simmer for 30 minutes, liquidize, and season to taste.
5. Meanwhile, season the chicken wings and roast in the preheated oven for 20-25 minutes until brown.
6. Reheat the sauce, pour over the wings, and sprinkle with a little chopped parsley.

Everybody lends a hand to make sure Coronation Street parties are a success. Usually it's Betty who has to organize the kitchen.

WHOLE SALMON

Serves 20-30 as part of a buffet
BAY LEAF
SPRIG OF PARSLEY AND THYME
1 ONION, SLICED
1 CARROT, PEELED AND CHOPPED
1/8 PINT/75ML WINE VINEGAR
SALT AND PEPER
1 WHOLE SALMON, ABOUT 7LB/3.2KG

1. Add the herbs, vegetables, wine vinegar, salt and pepper to a litre of water and simmer for 30-40 minutes. Strain the liquid and leave to get cold.
2. Scrape the scales off the salmon with the back of a knife.
3. If the fishmonger hasn't already done it, take out the gills and clean out the head. Then remove the intestines and clear the blood from the backbone.
4. Cut off the fins.
5. Wash the fish well and put in a fish kettle, or very large saucepan.
6. Cover the fish with the cold liquid.
7. Bring slowly to the boil, skim the surface and then simmer very gently for 20 minutes.
8. Leave the salmon in the liquid until cold.
9. Put the fish on a clean tea towel and carefully remove the skin.
10. You can serve the fish on a bed of lettuce, or you can cover it with mayonnaise and decorate with thin slices of cucumber if you're feeling artistic.

MUSTARD PORK ROAST

Serves 20 as part of a buffet
5LB/2.3KG LOIN OF PORK, BONED AND ROLLED
2 TABLESPOONS/30ML MADE MUSTARD
BROWN SUGAR
SALT AND PEPPER

1. Preheat the oven to 240°C/475°F/gas mark 8.
2. Take the skin off the pork and season with salt and pepper.
3. Spread the mustard all over the pork.
4. Sprinkle with sugar.
5. Roast in the oven for 20 minutes, then turn down the oven to 190°C/375°F/gas mark 5 for 3 hours, basting every so often.

FANCY BAKED POTATOES

Serves 10
10 MEDIUM-SIZED POTATOES
1 ONION
1OZ/30G BUTTER
4OZ/110G LANCASHIRE CHEESE
1 SMALL DOUBLE CARTON OF CREAM
1 EGG
SALT AND PEPPER
4OZ/110G MUSHROOMS

1. Preheat the oven to 200°C/400°F/gas mark 6.
2. Scrub the potatoes and bake in the oven until soft, about 1 hour.
3. Let them cool down a bit, then slice in half and scoop out the potato with a teaspoon, making sure you keep the skins intact.
4. Chop the onion very finely and fry gently in the butter until soft.
5. Mash the potato and mix in the onion.
6. Crumble in the cheese and stir well.
7. Beat the egg into the cream with plenty of salt and pepper and then mix it into the potato mixture.
8. Divide the mixture between the potato skins.
9. Slice the mushrooms and use to decorate the tops of the potatoes.
10. Return the potatoes to the oven and let them brown before serving.

HINDLE WAKES CHICKEN

Serves 10 as part of a buffet
8OZ/225G PRUNES, SOAKED OVERNIGHT AND STONED
2OZ/55G WHITE BREADCRUMBS
1 LARGE ONION, CHOPPED
1 TABLESPOON/15ML DRIED MIXED HERBS
1 TABLESPOON/15ML BROWN SUGAR
1OZ/30G SUET
SALT AND PEPPER
4LB/1.8KG CHICKEN
1/4 PINT/150ML WINE VINEGAR
1OZ/30G BUTTER
1OZ/30G FLOUR
1 TABLESPOON/15ML LEMON JUICE
GRATED LEMON AND ORANGE RIND
FINELY CHOPPED PARSLEY

1. Reserve 4 prunes for decorating the bird. Chop the rest and put in a bowl.
2. Add the breadcrumbs, onion, herbs, sugar and suet. Mix thoroughly and season to taste.
3. Use the prune mixture to stuff the chicken .
4. Put the chicken in large pan of water with vinegar and a pinch of salt.
5. Bring slowly to the boil, cover and simmer gently for around 2 hours or until tender.
6. Allow the chicken to cool in its cooking liquid. Skim the liquid when cold.
7. Remove the chicken from the pan and save 3/4 pint/425ml of the cooking liquid.
8. Carefully remove the skin from the bird.
9. Melt the butter in a saucepan and stir in the flour. Cook for 1 minute, stirring.
10. Take the pan off the heat and slowly stir in the reserved cooking liquid.
11. Return the pan to the heat and keep stirring until the sauce is smooth.
12. Add the lemon juice and cook for another minute.
13. Cover the bird with the sauce and sprinkle with the grated peel.
14. Cut the reserved prunes in half and decorate the bird.
15. Put in the fridge until required.

Fancy baked potatoes are fun to make and even more fun to eat.

POTATO SALAD

Serves 20

5LB/2.3KG POTATOES

2 BUNCHES SPRING ONIONS

FOR THE DRESSING:

1/4 PINT/150ML OLIVE OIL

4 TABLESPOONS/60ML WHITE WINE VINEGAR, OR TO TASTE

2 TEASPOONS/10ML DRIED MUSTARD

1 TEASPOON/5ML SUGAR

SALT AND PEPPER

1. Peel the potatoes and cut into chunks. Boil in salted water until just cooked.
2. Finely chop the spring onions. Carefully mix the onions with the potatoes in a couple of large bowls.
3. Put all the dressing ingredients in a large screw-top jar and shake well.
4. Pour the dressing over the potato salad while the potatoes are still hot.
5. Leave the salad to cool. Turn the potatoes again just before serving.

GREEN SALAD

Serves 30

4 COS LETTUCES

2 BUNCHES SPRING ONIONS

1 CUCUMBER

FOR THE DRESSING:

1/4 PINT/150ML OLIVE OIL

4 TABLESPOONS/60ML WHITE WINE VINEGAR

2 TEASPOONS/10ML DRIED MUSTARD

1 TEASPOON/5ML SUGAR

SALT AND PEPPER

1. Wash and drain the lettuces.
2. Tear the leaves into large pieces and put into bowls.
3. Wash the onions and cucumber.
4. Chop the onions and slice the cucumber thinly. Divide between the bowls.
5. Put all the dressing ingredients into large screw-top jar and shake well.
6. Just before serving pour the dressing over the salad and mix it through. Alternatively, serve the dressing separately.

If you don't end up dancing, you haven't enjoyed yourself.

Some people never stray far from the food at a party.

TRIFLE

Serves 10

6 TRIFLE SPONGES
RASPBERRY JAM
1 MEASURE BRANDY
1 MEASURE SHERRY
8OZ/225G RASPBERRIES, FRESH OR DEFROSTED FROZEN
1 BANANA
1/2 PINT/290ML CUSTARD
1 SMALL CARTON DOUBLE CREAM
2OZ/55G FLAKED ALMONDS

1. Spread the sponges with the jam and break them up into a glass bowl.

2. Sprinkle the sherry and brandy over the sponges.

3. Spread the raspberries and sliced bananas over the sponges.

4. Make the custard and allow to cool. Pour in a layer over the fruit and sponges.

5. Whip the cream and spread it over the custard.

6. Decorate with the almonds.

7. Cover and put in the fridge for a few hours before serving.

DES'S PASTA DELIGHT

I CAN SURVIVE ON TAKEAWAYS, things on toast or anything that's going, but there's one occasion when it's worth making that little bit of effort. A romantic evening in with the woman you fancy. A wonderful meal won't half impress her. And if you're going to impress her you might as well be around when it's all happening instead of stuck in the kitchen shouting through the door to her. Nearly everything in this meal is done in advance, leaving you just the last-minute touches to see to when you want to serve it. I've always found it works a treat.

COURGETTE SOUP

1 SMALL ONION, CHOPPED
1OZ/30G BUTTER
1LB/450G COURGETTES
1¼ PINTS/730ML WATER OR CHICKEN STOCK (SEE PAGE 10)
PEPPER
½ LARGE CARTON DOUBLE CREAM (USE THE OTHER HALF FOR THE PASTA SUPREME)
2OZ/55G LANCASHIRE CHEESE
SALT
PARSLEY

Before she arrives:
1. Cook the chopped onion gently in the butter, but don't let it brown.
2. Add the sliced courgettes and keep stirring as they cook.
3. Add the stock or water and a little pepper and simmer for 15-20 minutes.
4. Remove from the pan, let it cool slightly and liquidize.

When you want it:
5. Add the cream and cheese and heat through without boiling.
6. Sprinkle a little chopped parsley and swirl a teaspoon of cream on the surface of the soup.
7. Only serve small portions of the soup or you might both get too full to move.

Des's cooking usually works on one guest but he has no chance with both Steph and Raquel.

PASTA SUPREME

The secret for this one is to prepare everything in advance, then all you have to do is throw it together and serve.

OIL
SALT
8OZ/225G DRIED PASTA SHAPES
4OZ/110G MIXED SALAMI (USE AT LEAST 2 KINDS)
2OZ/55G SMOKED BACON
WHITE WINE
¾ PINT/425ML CHICKEN STOCK (SEE PAGE 10)
½ LARGE CARTON DOUBLE CREAM
SEASONING
CHOPPED PARSLEY

Before she arrives:
1. In a big pot add a little oil to lots of boiling salted water. This stops the pasta sticking together.
2. Add the pasta and stir once. Follow the directions on the packet for the cooking time, but test it.
3. When the pasta is just cooked, pour it into a sieve and put under the cold tap to stop it cooking. Put to one side.
4. Finely chop the bacon and salami. Fry the bacon to release the fat and then add the chopped salami. When cooked push the meats to one side of the pan and tilt the pan so that all the fat runs out of the meats. Carefully put the meats to one side with the pasta.
5. Leave everything next to the cooker, ready to use.

When you want it:
6. When you're ready to eat put a good measure of wine into a pan with the stock. Bring to the boil. Let it reduce a bit and add the cream. Do not let it boil again, or the cream will curdle. Season to taste.
7. Add the meats and stir.
8. Add the pasta and stir while it heats through.
9. Sprinkle with chopped parsley and serve.

Des is odds-on favourite to win the heart of any dinner guest.

CHEESE PLATE AND FRUIT

Before she arrives:
1. Get 2 kinds of cheese. Slice them and arrange on 2 plates.
2. Put a small bunch of grapes on each plate.
3. Place some cheese biscuits and butter on the plates.

When you want it:
4. Slice an apple thinly and add to the plates. Don't do this beforehand as the apple will discolour.

By the time you get to this point relations should be getting quite interesting, otherwise you might as well give up and go down the Rovers. Assuming things are fine, serve coffee and a liqueur. Any kind will do but make sure you serve it in a small glass. Half a tumbler of Cointreau won't go down very well at all.

From here on you're on your own.

Good luck!

DES BARNES

Left: Des has tried his best to get over Steph leaving him but he's found it very hard.
Above: Raquel went to a great deal of trouble organizing a surprise party for Des but it all started to go wrong when Steph's new man, Simon, turned up looking for her.

DES AND STEPH BARNES moved into No. 6 Coronation Street on their wedding night in 1990. Steph's father, Maurice Jones, had built the house and sold it to the couple at cost. They soon made their mark on the street. She was a bit wild and he followed her example. Their practical jokes didn't make them very popular with some of the residents. Derek and Mavis, in particular, didn't approve of some of the goings-on next door. Steph worked as a shop assistant on a perfume counter. When she got a part-time job doing promotions in pubs Des didn't like the customers ogling her skimpy costume and trying to chat her up. Des decided to build a boat in the back garden and this gradually caused a rift with Steph. He was so busy on the boat he didn't have time to take her out. By the time he had finished the boat Steph was having an affair with Simon and it was too late to save their marriage.

Since Steph left, Des has had a few quick romances but none have lasted. His affair with Raquel looked promising but when Steph briefly returned it all fell apart.

SALLY AND KEVIN'S CHILDREN'S PARTY

I'M VERY LUCKY HAVING KEVIN to help as he really does his share of work with the kids. I'm also pretty used to organizing parties or at least helping out, as between me and Gail we manage to have lots of them.

If you mention kids' parties to most parents they'll tell you they love other people's and hate their own. But they don't have to be that bad for the adults. All you've got to do is be strict on timing and organization. Then at the end of it you can just be thankful it's over for another year.

When parents drop their kids off make sure they know exactly when to pick them up. Make it clear that this is an exact time. It doesn't mean that little Johnnie is OK for another half hour or so after that time. If you haven't had a children's party before, then be advised that a couple of hours is ample time to have fun. More than that can quickly turn into a nightmare.

The party-goers are often too excited to eat much but it's a good idea to try and get something in them. You'll always find one kiddie who won't eat anything, but crisps are a good bet if all else fails.

Serve the sandwiches and sausage rolls before revealing the cakes and jellies, or you've no chance of getting anybody to eat anything savoury. Little sausages on sticks are easy to make and you can stick a load into half a potato and call it a hedgehog. Do the same with little cubes of cheese.

Jelly and ice cream are still as popular as ever. Get lots of small paper cases to serve jelly in. Use the cake mix to make lots of little cakes. Stick a cherry on top of each one.

There's not a lot of point trying to do everything posh as it won't last five minutes once

the kids get at it. Try and arrange everything so it's easier for you. The kids will survive the party. You might not.

Games are important. Don't have too many different kinds. It doesn't matter if you play pass the parcel for ages as long as everybody gets the chance to unwrap the parcel at least once. Young kids don't notice that the person controlling the music can see where the parcel's up to. So it's pretty easy to make sure everybody goes home happy. If you've got definite boy and girl prizes, colour code the wrapping paper so you can make sure they don't go to the wrong sex. Musical chairs or statues are both very popular and all ages enjoy a dance. Dancing is probably better when you've run out of things to do and you're desperate as you can keep it going to fill the time that you've got.

Don't forget that everybody should have something to take home with them. It used to be a slice of birthday cake and maybe a balloon if you were lucky. These days people provide surprise bags of little presents that are getting more and more expensive. Strike a blow for sanity and ignore the trend. Get back to the cake and balloons.

At the best kids' parties everybody gets to have a go at blowing out the candles.

GINGERBREAD MEN AND WOMEN

Makes about 20 depending on size of men and women
8OZ/225G PLAIN FLOUR
4OZ/110G BROWN SUGAR
2 TEASPOONS/10ML GROUND GINGER
1 TEASPOON/5ML CARAWAY SEEDS
1 TEASPOON/5ML CINNAMON
4OZ/110G BUTTER
2OZ/55G TREACLE
MILK

1. Preheat the oven to 150°C/300°F/gas mark 2.
2. Sift the flour and mix all the dry ingredients together in a basin.
3. Cream the butter and mix in with the ingredients in the basin until it resembles breadcrumbs.
4. Heat the treacle and add to the basin.
5. Knead to a stiff paste.
6. Add a little milk if it's too dry to roll out.
7. Roll out as thinly as possible and cut to shape. If you have any animal biscuit cutters use them.
8. Place on greased paper in a baking tin and bake for 10-15 minutes.
9. Remove from the oven and cool on a wire rack.

LITTLE SAUSAGE ROLLS

Makes 24
1LB/450G PUFF PASTRY
1LB/450G SAUSAGEMEAT

1. Preheat the oven to 200°C/400°F/gas mark 6.
2. Roll out the pastry to $^1/_8$ inch/0.25cm thick and 4 inches/10cm wide.
3. Make the sausagemeat into a roll 1 inch/2.5cm in diameter.
4. Place in the centre of the pastry.
5. Moisten the edges of the pastry and bring it over the sausagemeat. Seal it by pressing the edges together (make sure the join is on the underneath).
6. Cut into 24 sausage rolls.
7. Brush with a little milk and cut a little 'V' in the top of each roll. Bake for about 20 minutes or until golden brown.

CHOCOLATE MOUSSE

Serves 8
12OZ/340G PLAIN CHOCOLATE
1OZ/30G BUTTER
6 EGGS
VANILLA ESSENCE

1. Place a bowl over a pan of gently simmering water.
2. Put a spoonful of water with the chocolate into the bowl to melt the chocolate. Stir it, adding the butter.
4. Separate the eggs.
5. Take the basin off the heat and add the egg yolks and a couple of drops of vanilla essence and stir well.
6. Beat the egg whites stiff and fold into the chocolate.
7. Pour into 8 individual serving dishes and refrigerate.

BIRTHDAY CAKE

4OZ/110G SELF-RAISING FLOUR
1 TEASPOON/5ML BAKING POWDER
4OZ/110G SOFT MARGARINE
4OZ/110G CASTER SUGAR
1 TABLESPOON/15ML COCOA POWDER
2 LARGE EGGS
JAM
FOR THE ICING:
1LB/450G ICING SUGAR
2 EGG WHITES
$^1/_2$ TEASPOON/2.5ML LEMON JUICE
1 TEASPOON/5ML GLYCERINE

1. Turn the oven on to 170°C/325°F/gas mark 3.
2. Sift the flour and baking powder into a mixing bowl.
3. Add the rest of the ingredients except for the jam and whisk them together.
4. Divide between two 7 inch/18cm round or 6 inch/15cm square greased baking tins lined with greaseproof paper.
5. Bake for 30 minutes until springy to the touch.
6. Turn out on to a wire rack to cool.
7. Peel off the paper and sandwich together with jam.
8. Beat together the icing ingredients for 5 minutes with a wooden spoon until they go glossy.
9. Heat a little jam with a smaller amount of water and brush on the cake.
10. Quickly ice the cake. Don't forget the birthday candles!

Kevin and Sally Webster

Marriage and motherhood have mellowed Sally from the feisty young woman Kev first knew. The daughter of a timid mother and violent father, she's determined to give her own daughter, Rosie, the best family life possible. She wants more children but Kev wants to wait until they're more financially secure.

Brian Tilsley gave Kev a good training as a motor mechanic. Now Kevin is in charge at MVB Motors, but with quixotic Mike Baldwin at the helm he can never be totally sure where he stands. Sally combined her love of children with business sense by setting up as a Registered Child Minder for Gail's children.

The attentions of flirty Steph Barnes caused some friction when she persuaded Kev to shave off his moustache at a party. On the whole, though, theirs is a happy marriage and they look forward to a future surrounded by friends and a brood of little Websters.

Kids' parties aren't just for the kids. Kevin and Sally also know how to enjoy themselves.

RAQUEL'S SLIMMING TIPS

IT'S NOT EASY BEING A MODEL, as you have to watch what you eat all the time. You might feel really hungry and just want to put the chip pan on and really make a pig of yourself but you can't. You've got to have discipline. That's where a lot of girls fall down. They haven't got a system. They think they can just have the best of intentions and everything will work out fine. Well it doesn't. You've got to work at it. You've got to decide. Do you seriously want to look your best? If you do then you've got to do something about it. Here's my way. It gets a lot easier once you get into the swing of it. You get into the habit of resisting temptation – at least for food.

The first thing you have to understand is that it's no use letting yourself go and then trying a sudden crash diet in the hope that you'll lose loads of weight overnight. You have to change your normal way of eating so that it's better all the time. It's no use trying daft diets that involve eating nothing but bananas for three months or drinking three pints of carrot juice every day. You've got to find a way of eating that you enjoy. That way you'll stick at it.

I have general rules that cover everything. Once you get the hang of them you can eat all kinds of things depending on what's available, so you don't have to buy anything special. And once it gets into a routine, you'll quickly notice the benefits when your shape changes.

RAQUEL'S RULES

1. When you get up in the morning have a glass of hot water with a slice of lemon in it. It cleanses your system and is good for your skin. Try and drink a lot of water every day.

2. I know it's very difficult when you're out in other people's houses but keep coffee and tea down to a minimum. At home I drink herbal tea when I can as it contains no caffeine, which is bad for the skin.

3. I always use semi-skimmed milk. I'd use fully skimmed but I can't get used to it as it's so thin. I allow myself half a pint a day, which is for everything, including drinks and cereals.

4. I never eat butter. I do use a low-fat spread (high in polyunsaturates) when I can't avoid it, but I use as little as possible.

5. Cakes, biscuits, toffees and sweets are out! If you fancy a snack have some fruit, but don't eat grapes or bananas as they're high in calories. You can also have a carton of low-fat natural yoghurt, which is filling but not fattening.

6. Never eat fried food. Always grill it.

7. If you feel peckish you can always have a cup of Bovril or Oxo.

Raquel is very popular in the Rovers. Some customers travel miles just to buy a pint off her.

8. I'm sorry, pies are definitely out, which is bad news for Jack and Vera, but they're much too high in calories.

9. If you like cheese stick to Edam, which has fewer calories than other cheeses. For a special treat look out for low-fat versions of other cheeses.

10. Try and get some exercise. If all you do is slump in front of the telly every night you've got a problem. If you can't change your ways, then at least stop using the remote control to change channels. You don't have to start training for the Olympics: a little bit of walking will do you a world of good. Try doing some window-shopping on a Saturday morning.

RAQUEL'S EVERYDAY EATING

Breakfast
You can have a choice of 3 different breakfasts.
1. A small bowl of cereal: muesli, All-bran or Shreddies with no added sugar. Add some chopped fruit and use milk from your daily allowance.
2. A slice of wholemeal toast thinly spread with low-fat spread and honey.
3. A small carton of low-fat natural yoghurt and an apple.

Lunchtime
Have a sandwich made with brown bread containing a slice of meat and salad or just a salad, but try and keep it

Ring the changes with your salads or you'll get bored.

interesting by chopping up different raw vegetables and adding some nuts and raisins if you're not including any protein from meat, cheese or eggs.

Cottage cheese is a wonderful alternative to meat as it's full of protein and very low in calories.

Don't put mayonnaise on salad unless it's the low-calorie type but even then it's better to use none at all.

Evening meal

Grilled meat or fish is fine and if you're stuck for time fish fingers are OK.

Once a week try and have some grilled liver because it's full of iron. Don't fry it, of course.

Also once a week have some oily fish like sardines as this is a good source of vitamin A, which is good for the complexion.

You can have a baked potato with your meal, but don't put butter on it. If you like, you can have a baked potato with cottage cheese as your main meal.

A little salad always makes the meal more interesting. One of my favourites is grated carrot soaked in orange juice. It goes lovely with liver.

Always remember that you're supposed to enjoy your food, so vary it as much as possible. Don't eat the same thing night after night. You'll only get fed up with it.

SURVIVAL GUIDE TO EATING OUT

One big problem everybody has is what to eat if somebody asks you out. There's no point being in a restaurant if you're going to sit there and say you can't eat anything on the menu. If you know what you want, you can usually get it in most sensible restaurants, even if it's not on the menu. Here's what I usually order:

Starters

Fruit juice, melon, grapefruit, clear soup, smoked salmon, oysters or parma ham and melon. Never have pâté, thick soup, or avocado, which is very fattening.

Main Meal

Grilled fish without sauce, seafood without mayonnaise, steak cooked medium to well done, an omelette other than cheese. Most vegetables are fine apart from cauliflower cheese and sweetcorn.

Desserts

Fresh fruit, fruit sorbet or crème caramel.

Alcohol

Dry white wine or dry sherry are best. Dry Martini with ice and lemon is pretty good, and if you add low-cal tonic you've got a good long drink. Avoid liqueurs after a meal. If you must, then whisky is the best. If you can stick to low-calorie soft drinks that's the best plan of all, and don't nibble nuts or crisps when you're at the bar. They're full of calories.

Raquel confirmed her potential as a model when she became Miss Bettabuys, but unfortunately her career failed to blossom.

RAQUEL WOLSTENHULME

Raquel's been trained by experts. It's not easy to get Alec and Bet's seal of approval.

WHEN RAQUEL FIRST APPEARED on the street she was working in Bettabuys and both Curly and Reg were captivated by her charms. She was voted Miss Bettabuys and went on to compete in the Miss Bettabuys North-West Regional Final. Although she didn't win, it confirmed that Raquel had a promising career as a model ahead of her. After modelling Angie's design collection for the Polytechnic show, a photographer employed her to model lingerie. She began to drift apart from Curly and finished with him, telling him they were moving in different circles. She left The Street, confident that she was going to make it big in modelling. Unfortunately it didn't work out.

When she returned Angie put her up for the night and was rewarded by Raquel pinching Des off her and moving into his house. She got a job in the Rovers and her relationship with Des blossomed. But it all crumbled when Steph returned and Des thought he had a chance of resurrecting his marriage.

JIM'S CAFÉ

GAIL AND ALMA PROVIDE many delights for the inhabitants of Coronation Street. From breakfast to a full meal or just somewhere to sit and gossip over a cup of tea. You can find it all at Jim's Café. If you're really lucky, you might find yourself on the same table as Percy Sugden, or even be served by Phyllis, but at least the food will always be good. Here are three of the customers' all-time favourite dishes.

SHEPHERD'S PIE

Serves 4

1LB/450G MINCED LAMB

1 ONION, FINELY CHOPPED

OIL

1 TEASPOON/5ML FLOUR

1/2 PINT/290ML BEEF STOCK (SEE PAGE 10)

PINCH OF MIXED HERBS

SALT AND PEPPER

1LB/450G MASHED POTATOES

BUTTER

1. Preheat the oven to 180°C/350°F/gas mark 4.

2. Fry the minced lamb and finely chopped onion in the oil in a large frying pan until browned.

3. Remove the meat and onion mixture and place in a saucepan. Add the flour and cook, stirring, for 30 seconds.

4. Add the stock, mixed herbs, salt and pepper, and slowly bring to the boil, stirring all the time.

5. Put the meat in a pie dish, keeping back some of the liquid if the mixture is very runny. Leave to cool slightly and then cover with the mashed potatoes. Dot the top with butter.

6. Bake in the oven for 45 minutes or until golden brown.

Left: Gail and Alma run the café with a smile. Above: Phyllis is always willing to help – even if nobody wants her to!

Although it's made from the simplest of ingredients bread and butter pudding has remained a firm favourite with Gail and Alma's customers.

BREAD AND BUTTER PUDDING

Serves 6

6 SLICES WHITE BREAD

2OZ/55G BUTTER

4 EGGS

2OZ/55G SUGAR

3/4 PINTS/425ML MILK

1/2OZ/15G CURRANTS

1/2OZ/15G SULTANAS

1/2OZ/15G CHOPPED MIXED PEEL

GRATED NUTMEG

1. Preheat the oven to 180°C/350°F/gas mark 4.

2. Remove the crusts from the bread, butter and cut the slices into triangles.

3. Beat the eggs with the sugar.

4. Heat the milk gently, without boiling, pour into the eggs and mix well.

5. Mix together the currants, sultanas and chopped peel. Spread half this mixture over the bottom of a buttered pie dish.

6. Place half the bread on top and then the rest of the dried-fruit mixture.

7. Pour half the egg and milk mixture over the bread and let it soak in for a few minutes.

8. Arrange the rest of the bread on top of this and pour over the rest of the custard.

9. Grate some nutmeg over the surface of the pudding.

10. Bake for 45 minutes or until the custard is set and the top is crusty and brown.

COCONUT PUDDING

Serves 4-6

2OZ/55G MARGARINE

8OZ/225G WHITE SUGAR

4 EGGS

4OZ/110G SELF-RAISING FLOUR, SIEVED

1/2 TEASPOON/2.5ML BAKING POWDER

PINCH OF SALT

1 PINT/570ML MILK

8OZ/225G DESICCATED COCONUT

1 TEASPOON/5ML VANILLA ESSENCE

1. Preheat the oven to 180°C/350°F/gas mark 4.

2. Mix all ingredients together in a bowl in the order given above, mixing well after every addition.

3. Pour into a 10 inch buttered dish and bake for 1 hour.

ALMA BALDWIN

There can't be many cafés with as attractive a proprietor as Alma.

ALMA HAS sometimes seemed to be one of life's victims, careering from one disastrous affair to another – more often than not involving Mike Baldwin somewhere along the line. Yet she is also a major partner in Jim's Café, which she and Gail run successfully, though it's taken Gail ten years to 'train' Alma into doing an equal share of the work. At times, Mike has treated Alma abominably but she has consistently bailed him out, even turning her hand to sewing travel bags when he was on his uppers.

When Mike left her for Jackie Ingram she got involved with Ken Barlow. He fell for her heavily but on New Year's Eve left her stranded in a hotel when she confessed she'd spent Christmas Day in bed with Mike.

She finally agreed to marry Mike and they settled comfortably into married life, though Mike knows he can't take advantage of her any more. These days Alma is nobody's fool.

ANGIE'S CHEAP AND CHEERFUL

I LEARNT TO MAKE most of these recipes when I was a student because like all students I never had any money. Usually it was a choice between buying food or materials for my degree course. But I did manage to survive and even though I've got a job now and enough money to eat what I want I still make the same dishes because they taste pretty good. None of them have meat in them because I could never afford meat but some of them are improved by using chicken stock rather than water, although it isn't essential. You can use chicken stock cubes or make your own like Betty does.

I think one of the triumphs of my time with Curly has been forcing him to do his share of the cooking. Some of his efforts have been disgusting but I've forced myself to eat them on principle. I like to think that as a result of my efforts I've made him a better person.

Just remember that you don't have to spend a lot of money to eat well. You just have to think about it for a minute or two. All these recipes are cheap, cheerful and most of all delicious.

LENTIL SOUP

Serves 4
4oz/110g lentils (red, brown or green)
1 large onion
a little oil
1 large carrot
1 clove of garlic
1 small tin of chopped tomatoes
1³/4 pints/1 litre chicken stock (see page 10) or water
salt and pepper

1. Put the lentils on a plate and swirl them round so you can pick out any that are black or discoloured or any tiny stones.
2. Put the lentils in a pan and swirl them round under the cold tap to wash them.
3. In a large saucepan, fry the chopped onion gently in the oil until soft but not brown.
4. Add the peeled and chopped carrot and stir.
5. Add the lentils and stir.
6. Add the chopped garlic.
7. Add the tomatoes and stock and a little salt and pepper.
8. Cover and cook gently for about 45-60 minutes. Stir every so often to stop it sticking.

POTATO AND LEEK SOUP

Serves 4
1lb/450g leeks
1 large onion
1oz/30g butter
1lb/450g potatoes
2 pints/1.14 litres water or mixture of water
and chicken stock (see page 10)
salt and pepper

1. Clean the leeks by slitting them lengthways and holding them under a running cold tap. Chop them finely.
2. Chop the onion finely.
3. Fry the onion and leek gently in the butter until soft.
4. Peel the potatoes and chop into smallish chunks.
5. Add the potatoes to the leek and onions along with the water or chicken stock and water mixture and simmer for approximately 25 minutes.
6. Liquidize the soup or mash the potaoes so that they disintegrate.
7. Taste it and add seasoning.

Left: Artistic Angie has put her talents to great use in the Street, but she's had no success redesigning Curly.

It may be just macaroni cheese to you, but Angie manages to turn it into something new and exciting.

CHEESEY POTATOES

You can add things like a few mushrooms or a finely sliced carrot but it's just as good done simple.

Serves 6
2OZ/55G BUTTER
I LARGE ONION
I CLOVE OF GARLIC
2LB/900G POTATOES
SALT AND PEPPER
1/2 PINT/290ML MILK
3OZ/85G LANCASHIRE CHEESE

1. Preheat the oven to 200°C/400°F/gas mark 6.
2. Butter a baking dish with half the butter.
3. Finely chop the onion and the garlic.
4. Peel and thinly slice the potatoes.
5. Sprinkle the garlic on the bottom of the dish, then put a layer of onion followed by a layer of potato and repeat, finishing with a layer of potato.
6. Season the milk with salt and pepper and mix

thoroughly. Pour over the dish. Dot with the rest of the butter.
7. Cover tightly or seal with foil and bake for I hour.
8. Uncover the dish, sprinkle with the crumbled cheese and bake for a further 10 minutes or so until the top browns.
9. This will keep in the oven while you're sorting out other things and you can serve it as a main dish or as a vegetable with other main dishes.

TUNA MACARONI CHEESE

Serves 2
3OZ/85G MACARONI
I OZ/30G BUTTER
I OZ/30G FLOUR
1/2 PINT/290ML MILK
3OZ/85G LANCASHIRE CHEESE
SALT AND PEPPER
I SMALL TIN TUNA
I TABLESPOON/15ML BREADCRUMBS

1. Cook the macaroni for 10-15 minutes in boiling water and drain.
2. Make a cheese sauce: melt the butter, stirring in the flour until it goes golden coloured, then bring the pan off the heat and very gradually add the milk, stirring all the time.
3. Put the pan back on to the heat and carry on stirring and simmering until the sauce thickens.
4. Remove from the heat and add two-thirds of the cheese and stir while it melts. Season with salt and pepper.
5. Drain the tuna and flake it with a fork. Add to the sauce, mixing in well.
6. Add the macaroni to the sauce and mix well. Pour into a baking dish.
7. Sprinkle the rest of the cheese and the breadcrumbs over the dish and brown it under a hot grill.

ANGIE FREEMAN

Angie's career as a barmaid ended after she poured a pint of beer over Des's head.

AFTER A SPELL in Canterbury, Angie returned to her native Manchester to study Fashion Design at the Poly, where Flick Khan introduced her to Jenny Bradley. Sharing No. 7 Coronation Street had its ups and downs before Jenny finally ran away with a married man – to Angie's disapproval. Curly then moved in, but Angie's forthright manner and feminist leanings put a stop to any speculation. With the odd embarrassing lapse, they've kept things platonic ever since.

In the full flush of a romance with Des Barnes, Angie took pity on Curly and reunited him with Raquel – only to watch Raquel stroll off into the sunset with Des by her side. Angie wisely decided her time would be better spent on her studies and, with a good degree under her belt, was taken on as a buyer for up-and-coming Onyx Designs. She seems destined for success in her career – if not in her relationships with men, who so rarely match up to her high principles and sardonic sense of humour.

CURLY'S CULINARY CREATIONS

EVEN THOUGH IT MEANS WORKING for Reg Holdsworth, I must admit that there are advantages to being employed by Bettabuys. All the world is there. Whatever I need in the way of ingredients is always available. Unless, of course, we've sold out and I've forgotten to reorder. But I've always been a bit adventurous in my cooking, so here I've included dishes from France, India and South America. Needless to say, if you want to try any of them, you can get all the ingredients very cheaply at your local Bettabuys.

CHICKEN IN RED WINE

Serves 2
2OZ/55G RAISINS
1/4 BOTTLE RED WINE
2 CHICKEN BREASTS
BUTTER
OIL
I RASHER STREAKY BACON
I ONION
I CLOVE OF GARLIC
1/4 PINT/150ML STOCK OR WATER
2OZ/55G MUSHROOMS
2 TABLESPOONS/30ML DOUBLE CREAM

1. Soak the raisins in the wine.
2. Brown the chicken breasts on both sides in a little butter and oil and remove from the pan.
3. Chop the bacon and fry it gently in the pan.
4. Slice the onion and add to the pan, stirring until it softens.
5. Add the chopped garlic and stir into the onions.
6. Add the wine and raisins and bring to the boil, simmering for a minute or two.
7. Add the stock and sliced mushrooms.
8. Put the chicken back in the pan, cover and simmer for 45 minutes until the chicken is tender.
9. Stir in the cream and heat through.
10. Serve with rice or boiled potatoes and drink the rest of the wine with the dish.

Curly doesn't like any cooking that is over-elaborate, but he's a dab hand with the old favourites.

CHICKEN CURRY

Serves 2
4 CHICKEN THIGHS
I ONION
I CARROT
2 TEASPOONS/10ML CURRY POWDER
I RED CHILLI, DESEEDED
3/4 PINT/425ML CHICKEN STOCK (SEE PAGE 10)
1/2 TEASPOON/2.5ML TURMERIC
I CLOVE GARLIC
1OZ/30G DESICCATED COCONUT

1. Chop the chilli finely. (Wash your hands carefully afterwards.)
2. Chop the onion and fry it gently in a little oil. Add the peeled and chopped carrot.
3. Add the chopped garlic, the curry powder and the turmeric.
4. Roughly chop the chicken and season with salt and pepper.
5. Add the chicken to the pan and stir it round, coating it with the spiced oil.
6. Add the chicken stock and coconut. Bring to the boil and simmer gently for 25-30 minutes.
7. Serve with boiled rice and mango chutney.

Note: If you like your curry hot, don't deseed the chilli.

CORNED BEEF HASH

Serves 2-3
2 ONIONS
OIL
8OZ/225G CORNED BEEF
1LB/450G BOILED POTATOES
WORCESTERSHIRE SAUCE
SALT AND PEPPER

1. Fry the chopped onions in a little oil until they're soft.
2. Chop the corned beef and potatoes into cubes and add them and the Worcestershire sauce to the pan.
3. Stir round, then fry gently for 20 minutes or so. The corned beef will release its fat but will eventually crisp up on the bottom. Either turn the mixture in the pan or slide it under the grill to brown the top.

CHILLI CON CARNE

Serves 2
1 LARGE ONION
OIL
1 CLOVE GARLIC
1 TEASPOON/5ML CHILLI POWDER
1 RASHER OF BACON
8OZ/225G STEWING STEAK OR MINCE
1 SMALL TIN CHOPPED TOMATOES
1/2 PINT/290ML STOCK OR WATER
SALT AND PEPPER
1 TIN RED KIDNEY BEANS
TABASCO SAUCE

1. Fry the chopped onion gently in a little oil until it's soft.
2. Add the chopped garlic and the chilli powder.
3. Chop the bacon finely and add to the pan with the chopped steak or mince.
4. Stir round while the meat colours, then add the tomatoes and the stock.
5. Bring to the boil, add salt and pepper, cover and simmer for 2 1/2 hours for stewing steak and 1 hour for mince. Add the kidney beans towards the end to heat through but not overcook.
6. Add salt and Tabasco sauce to taste.
7. Serve with boiled rice.

SPARE RIBS

1 LB/450G SPARE RIBS
1 CLOVE GARLIC
1 TABLESPOON/15ML TOMATO PURÉE
2 TABLESPOONS/30ML SOY SAUCE
1 TABLESPOON/15ML BROWN SUGAR
1 TABLESPOON/15ML MARMALADE
1 TEASPOON/5ML DRIED MUSTARD
1/4 PINT/150ML BOILING WATER
TABASCO SAUCE
PEPPER

1. Preheat the oven to 200°C/400°F/gas mark 6.
2. Finely chop the garlic and put it in a bowl with the soy sauce, the tomato purée and the boiling water.
3. Add the mustard powder, sugar and marmalade.
4. Add a few drops of Tabasco and some pepper.
5. Brush the spare ribs with the sauce and roast them in the oven for 30 minutes.

Note: If you like, you can marinade the ribs in the sauce overnight in the fridge.

They may not be the most efficient management team in the food industry, but they are definitely the funniest.

CURLY WATTS

Curly's dreams of Raquel were shattered when she left him to pursue her modelling career – but they still get on very well.

URLY'S MOTTO IS PROBABLY *per ardua ad astra* – by steep and toilsome ways to the stars. Having started life emptying bins, he's scaled the heady heights of management in the Bettabuys supermarket chain – with just a little astronomy thrown in for good measure.

Unfortunately, his love life has been more haphazard. He lived with Shirley Armitage for a year before his studies caused a rift. Bettabuys soon introduced him to the delights – and frustrations – of Kimberley Taylor and her monstrous parents. Egged on by his mentor, Reg Holdsworth, Curly eventually broke free of their stranglehold and sought solace with Miss Bettabuys, Raquel Wolstenhulme, until she dumped him for her modelling career. He then moved in with student Angie Freeman but she swiftly put the blocks on any romance.

After a hint from Area Manager, Brendan Scott, Curly decided he needed a mate and joined a dating agency. He was introduced to... Kimberley. Kimberley claimed that Fate and Science had conspired to reunite them. Reg continues to block Curly's advancement at every opportunity. Now a home owner and landlord to boot, Curly commands more respect from the Taylors but is beginning to suspect there's more to life than a warm pair of slippers and a decent greenhouse.

THE MCDONALDS' FAMILY FAVOURITES

I T'S NOT EASY FEEDING A FAMILY on a budget. It takes a lot of skill and hard work. Jim's always been a worker and needed feeding properly, and two growing lads can be a nightmare. But as a mother you've got to cope. These days the lads are a lot easier to feed, now that they don't have as many fads as they did when they were kids. But they still have their favourite foods, which you have to bear in mind if you don't want trouble...

Jim seems to think my Irish stew is pretty good but I've never dared ask him if it's as good as his mother's. I've put the recipe here and also a couple of the lads' favourites, burgers and toad in the hole. Jim insisted on doing his pasta dish, which he tells everybody is wonderful. What isn't wonderful is that he manages to dirty every pan in the house when he makes it at home.

I've also done a couple of my Rovers dishes which people seem to like a lot and want to be able to do at home.

BEEFBURGERS

This makes four good-sized burgers that are a million times tastier than bought-in ones.

Serves 4
1LB/450G MINCED BEEF
1 ONION
SALT AND PEPPER
DRIED MIXED HERBS
WORCESTER OR TABASCO SAUCE
1 EGG
FAT FOR FRYING

1. Put the mince in a bowl and add the finely chopped onion. Using a fork, mix well.
2. Add the salt and pepper, mixed herbs and Worcester or Tobasco sauce.
3. Beat the egg and use enough of it to bind the meat mixture.
4. Divide the mixture into four, shape each burger into a ball and then, using wet hands, flatten into rounds.
5. Fry the burgers over a medium heat for 10-15 minutes, turning occasionally.
6. Serve on a bun with chips and relish.

IRISH STEW

Serves 4
1 1/2LB/675G LEAN SCRAG END OR MIDDLE NECK OF LAMB
1 PINT/570ML OF WATER
2 ONIONS, SLICED
2 CARROTS, PEELED AND SLICED
DRIED MIXED HERBS
3LB/1.3KG POTATOES
SALT AND PEPPER

1. Trim the meat of fat and chop into even pieces.
2. Put in a pan with the water, bring to the boil, skim and simmer for 1 hour.
3. Add the onions, carrots and a pinch of mixed herbs to the meat.
4. Peel two of the potatoes and chop them into small pieces. Add to the pan and simmer for 30 minutes. These will slowly disintegrate and thicken the stew.
5. Peel the rest of the potatoes and cut into even-sized chunks. Add them to the pan.
6. Cover and simmer until cooked. Adjust seasoning and skim off any fat.

Liz McDonald's evening snacks have been a big success at the Rovers.

Toad in the hole doesn't cost much but it helps feed a growing family.

TOAD IN THE HOLE

Serves 4
8 SAUSAGES
4OZ/110G PLAIN FLOUR
SALT AND PEPPER
1 EGG
1/2 PINT/290ML MILK

1. Sift the flour with a good pinch of salt into a basin. Make a well in the centre and add the egg. Gradually draw the flour into the egg, slowly adding the milk until you have a smooth batter.
2. Leave to rest at room temperature for 30 minutes, which will help give a lighter result.
3. Heat the oven to 220°C/425°F/gas mark 7.
4. Put the sausages in the oven for 10 minutes or fry until brown but not cooked through.
5. Either put the sausages into one large tin and pour the batter over them, or do individual tins.
6. Bake for 20-25 minutes until the risen batter is brown.

Jim's cooking is often more enthusiastic than skilled, but at least he has a go.

JIM'S PASTA

1 RASHER OF STREAKY BACON
OIL
1 LARGE ONION
1 CLOVE OF GARLIC
8OZ/225G MINCED BEEF
1/2OZ/10G PLAIN FLOUR
14OZ/400G TIN OF CHOPPED TOMATOES
1/2 PINT/290ML WATER OR RED WINE
PINCH OF DRIED THYME
BAY LEAF
14OZ/400G DRIED PASTA SHAPES
SALT

1. Chop the bacon finely and fry in the oil until it begins to brown.
2. Finely chop the onion and garlic and add to the pan.
3. Stir while the onions soften.
4. Add the minced beef and break up with a wooden spoon.
5. When the meat is browned, add the flour and mix.
6. Add the tomatoes.
7. Add the water or wine, thyme and bay leaf.
8. Simmer for 30 minutes, stirring occasionally. Check seasoning.
9. Fill your biggest pan with boiling salted water. Add a spoonful of oil to the water and the pasta. Stir once and simmer until the pasta is cooked.
10. Drain the pasta and serve with the beef and tomato sauce.

Even though Jim had no intention of reporting the hotpot to the Public Health authorities, the threat struck terror into Alec's heart.

ROVERS SPECIAL STEAK BARM

Serves 1

FROZEN SANDWICH STEAK
1 ONION
SALT AND PEPPER
OIL
BARM CAKE
BUTTER

1. Use frozen sandwich steaks that you just peel off.
2. Fry the chopped onion in oil until it starts to brown. Add a little water to it and salt and pepper. Let it simmer for 20 minutes.
3. Smear a frying pan with a little oil and heat. Very quickly fry the steak.
4. Put the steak on the buttered barm cake with a spoonful of the onions.
5. Serve with tomato sauce if liked.

ROVERS BEEF CURRY

Serves 4-6

1LB/450G STEWING STEAK, TRIMMED AND CUT INTO PIECES
SALT AND PEPPER
OIL
2 ONIONS, CHOPPED
1 CLOVE OF GARLIC, CRUSHED
1/2OZ/15G CURRY POWDER
1/2OZ/15G FLOUR
1/2OZ/15G TOMATO PURÉE
1OZ/30G CHOPPED CHUTNEY
1/4OZ/7G DESICCATED COCONUT
1/2OZ/15G SULTANAS
1 PINT/570ML BEEF STOCK (SEE PAGE 10)

1. Season the meat and brown it quickly in the oil.
2. Add the onions and garlic to the pan. When they are soft, add the curry powder, stir and fry.
3. Add the flour and continue stirring. Mix in the tomato purée, chutney, coconut and sultanas. Stir in the hot stock.
4. Cover and simmer for 2 hours, until the meat is cooked.
5. Serve with plain boiled rice.

THE MCDONALDS

FATHER JIM, MOTHER LIZ and twin teenage sons Andy and Steve moved into The Street after years of moving around Europe as an army family. At first, Jim found it difficult to cope with civvy street and family life suffered. But the family were very much pulled together by the birth and then tragic early death of daughter Katherine. It took Liz a while to get over the loss, but with Jim increasingly supportive and the twins growing more mature and into adulthood, the McDonalds pulled each other through.

Jim is a brusque Irishman, who calls a spade a spade, enjoys a pint and can turn his hand to most anything. It's a good job he can, because his own motorbike repair shop folded thanks to the recession, and now he's earning his living as a security guard. Twins Andy and Steve are chalk and cheese. Andy's the more studious one, while there's a bit of the rebel in brother Steve. Liz is the calming influence within the family, and works over the road at The Rovers Return.

The McDonalds – two teenage boys and a husband aren't easy to feed, but Liz manages it.

ALF'S OFFAL

I'M NOT BEING CRITICAL but Audrey's a bit sensitive when it comes to food. In fact you could call her downright fussy. She won't cook black puddings or tripe and she won't even touch them when I cook them. To be honest there isn't a lot that Audrey *will* cook, so when I want to eat any of my favourites I have to do it myself. It's a pity more people don't follow my example because offal's very cheap and it provides some of the tastiest dishes you can eat. Audrey doesn't know what she's missing.

GRILLED BLACK PUDDINGS AND APPLE SAUCE

One black pudding per person is fine for a starter. Two each for a main dish, but remember that they are very rich.

FOR THE APPLE SAUCE:
1LB/450G COOKING APPLES
1/2OZ/15G BUTTER
APPLE JUICE OR CREAM
SUGAR TO TASTE

1. Make the apple sauce first. Slice the peeled, cored and quartered apples into the butter in a pan and simmer until they start to disintegrate. You can add a little apple juice or cream to thin it down or just use the apples. Taste it, as you may need to add a little sugar. You can serve this roughly whipped with a fork or if you want it really smooth you can liquidize it. I prefer it without liquidizing, but it's up to you. Audrey complains that I use every pot in the house when I cook so I suppose the liquidizer wouldn't make much difference but I like to make an effort.
2. Peel the skin off the black puddings and cut them in half lengthways. Put under a hot grill for a couple of minutes and make sure they're piping hot.
3. If you want this to be a posh starter fit for kings, put some of the hot apple sauce on to a plate. Arrange the slices of black pudding on top of the sauce. Sprinkle with a little chopped parsley as a garnish and serve.
4. If you're serving this as a main dish it's better to serve some plain vegetables such as boiled potatoes with it because of the richness.

Left: Alf's black puddings – the most wonderful food in the world.

BRAISED OXTAIL

This is a smashing winter dish that takes a fair bit of time to make but is well worth it in the end. It's best to make it the day before so you can let it cool down completely. That way it's easy to remove the fat from the surface. Otherwise, just spoon off as much of the fat as you can.

Serves 4
2 TABLESPOONS/30ML FLOUR
SALT AND PEPPER
1 LARGE OXTAIL CUT INTO PIECES
1 TABLESPOON/15ML OIL
2 ONIONS
2 CARROTS
1 1/2 PINTS/860ML BEEF STOCK
BAY LEAF
1 TEASPOON/5 ML DRIED THYME
1 TABLESPOON/15ML TOMATO PURÉE

1. Preheat the oven to 150°C/300°F/gas mark 2 (see step 5).
2. Season the flour with salt and pepper and coat the oxtail pieces with it. In a flame-proof casserole dish, brown the oxtail in the oil until it's a good strong colour. Remove the meat on to a plate when it has browned.
3. Chop the onions. If necessary, add a little more oil to the casserole and fry the onions, stirring them all the time until they soften. Add the roughly chopped carrots and fry them a little.
4. Add the stock, herbs and tomato purée. Add the meat and bring to a simmer.
5. Either cover and simmer on top of stove for 3 hours, or cover tightly and cook in the oven for 3 hours.
6. Remove any fat from the surface, or if you are going to reheat and eat the oxtail the next day, allow it to cool and then remove the fat.
7. Serve with boiled potatoes and cabbage.

Liver and bacon – food of the gods.

LAMBS' LIVER AND MUSHROOMS

Serves 4
1OZ/30G BUTTER
1 ONION
1LB/450G LAMBS' LIVER
FLOUR
4OZ/110G MUSHROOMS, CLEANED AND SLICED
1/4 PINT/150ML BEEF STOCK (SEE PAGE 10)
PINCH OF MIXED HERBS
4 TOMATOES, SKINNED AND CHOPPED
SMALL CARTON DOUBLE CREAM

1. Melt the butter and gently fry the onion until soft.
2. Cut the liver into strips and coat with flour.
3. Add the liver and mushrooms to the onions and fry for 5 minutes. Add the stock and herbs and bring to the boil.
4. Add the tomatoes and simmer for 5 minutes.
5. Add the cream and heat through without boiling. Season and serve with plain boiled potatoes or rice.

TRIPE AND ONIONS

Serves 1 (large helping)
8OZ/225G DRESSED TRIPE
1/2 PINT/290ML MILK
1 ONION
SALT AND PEPPER
1OZ/30G BUTTER
3/4OZ/20G PLAIN FLOUR
PARSLEY

1. Put the tripe in a pan and cover with cold water. Bring to the boil, then drain under cold running water.
2. Cut the tripe into small pieces and put in a pan with the milk, sliced onion, salt and pepper. Cover and simmer for 2 hours.
3. Strain off the liquid from the pan and use 1/2 pint of it to make a white sauce with the butter and flour (see page 11).
4. Add the tripe and onions to the sauce and serve sprinkled with chopped parsley.

After years as a shopkeeper, Alf has tried most kinds of food, but given the choice he'll always pick offal for himself.

Alf and Audrey for once show their true feelings for each other – but it won't last.

BLACK PUDDING OR LIVER AND RAISINS IN STOUT

You can use liver or black pudding for this recipe and red wine instead of stout if you like.

Serves 4-6

2 MEDIUM ONIONS
2OZ/55G BUTTER
1¹/₂LB /675G LAMBS' LIVER OR BLACK PUDDING, SLICED
1OZ/30G PLAIN FLOUR
2OZ/55G SEEDLESS RAISINS
¹/₂ TEASPOON/2.5ML DRIED THYME
¹/₂ PINT/290ML OF STOUT, OR RED WINE
1 PINT/570ML BEEF STOCK
SALT AND PEPPER

1. Preheat the oven to 180°C/350°F/gas mark 4.
2. Gently fry the finely sliced onions in butter until transparent.
3. Butter a wide shallow casserole. Dip the black pudding or liver slices in the flour and put half of them in the dish.
4. Put the onions on top and sprinkle over half the raisins and the thyme.
5. Top with the remaining black pudding or liver, onions, raisins and thyme.
6. Mix the stout or red wine with the beef stock, salt and pepper and pour into the casserole
7. Cover with foil and then a lid and cook for about 1¹/₂ hours for black pudding, ³/₄ hour for liver.

FRIED LIVER AND BACON WITH ONIONS

Serves 2

8OZ/225G POTATOES, PEELED
2 SMALL ONIONS
1OZ/30G BUTTER
8OZ/225G LAMBS' LIVER
2 RASHERS BACON

1. Boil the potatoes until tender.
2. Meanwhile slice the onions and fry for 3-4 minutes in half the butter.
3. Add the remaining butter, the sliced liver and bacon and continue to fry gently for 5 minutes.
4. Put the liver, bacon, and onions on a warm plate.
5. Add a little of the potato water to the juices in the frying pan, bring to the boil and stir. Pour over the liver and bacon and serve with the potatoes.

ALF ROBERTS

A STALWART of the local community, Alf has served his friends and neighbours as both Corner Shop proprietor and local councillor over the years. Back in 1973-74, he was even Mayor of Weatherfield, but these days, is just the representative for the local St Mary's ward – ironically, a seat he won from Deirdre Barlow, who now works behind the counter at the Corner Shop.

Married three times, he inherited the shop from his second wife, Renee, who died in a car crash. He tied the knot for a third time with Audrey, but it's not all been plain-sailing. Audrey hates working in the shop, and once even left him.

But after suffering a heart attack that nearly killed him, Alf has tried to take life much more easily – and Audrey's done her bit to make sure he doesn't over-work himself. In many ways, his ill-health has pulled them closer together.

As Weatherfield's grocer, Alf has to be one of the world's greatest experts on fine food.

AUDREY'S QUICK SNACKS

YOU MIGHT HAVE NOTICED that I'm not the world's greatest cook. Well, I'm not so bad if I put my mind to it, but I've always thought there are better things to do with my time than slaving over a hot stove all day. I think I'm probably better at eating stuff that other people have cooked. I'm always very grateful. It's important to encourage people who like to be domestic, otherwise they stop doing it. My Alfie's very keen on cooking, but he makes all these dreadful things. Offal! Awful, I say. Why he can't just like what normal people like I don't know.

I can't touch the stuff, so he's on his own most of the time. We eat separately quite a lot. Well, apart from the dreadful things he cooks, he's always off at Council meetings and dos, so I just make myself something quick. And by the time he gets in and starts putting the chip pan on to make what he calls a 'snack', I really can't face it.

So while Alfie's playing with his puddings, I just get on with it. There's an awful lot of things you can do on toast. It's quite amazing really. Mind you, I don't eat very much, and I'm not one of those who eats for comfort. It's not that I don't have sympathy for people who do, but there are limits. Some of the women I see in the Corner Shop, you wonder how they managed to get through the door.

I do seem to eat a lot of soup, but I'm not going to bother giving you any recipes. Let's face it, anybody can open a tin, can't they? But its incredible what you can do with a tin of creamed chicken if you put your mind to it.

Audrey has always had better things to do with her time than cooking. Watching the telly in bed is just one of her preferred pastimes.

BLT

My favourite toastie of all time is my BLT – bacon, lettuce and tomato. Ken Barlow tells me it's American but what's American about bacon, lettuce and tomato I don't know. Sounds very English to me. Sometimes I think Ken makes things up just so people think he's clever. I always think it's sad when people get like that, but I don't suppose they can help it really. They're just not very secure in themselves. Anyway, here's how to make it.

Serves 1

2 BACON RASHERS
3 SLICES OF BREAD
BUTTER
LETTUCE
MAYONNAISE
1 TOMATO
SALT AND PEPPER

1. Grill the bacon.
2. Toast the bread. For a change you could have it untoasted if you like, but try it this way for now.
3. Butter 1 slice and put a bit of lettuce on it.
4. Cover the lettuce with both rashers of bacon.
5. Butter another piece of toast and put it on top of the bacon.
6. Spread mayonnaise over this second piece of toast.
7. Cover with some more lettuce and then the thinly sliced tomatoes.
8. Give it a sprinkle of salt and pepper and then cover with the last round of toast.
9. Press it down and slice through into two triangles. A wonderful double-decker!

Sandwich variations are endless and its important to ring the changes every so often. All cheese and tomato every night makes Audrey a very dull girl! Liver sausage and cucumber is one of my favourites, and I do lots of different things with cans of salmon. If you eat a lot of toasted sandwiches it's worth getting one of those toastie machines. They keep everything sealed in and make it all a bit special.

Alf and Audrey don't always see eye to eye. Audrey certainly doesn't share Alf's love of offal.

POACHED EGG ON TOAST

Poached eggs are easy enough to do, even if you haven't got a proper poacher. Just bring a pan of water to the boil and add a tablespoonful of vinegar. Let the water simmer and stir it quite hard to make a little whirlpool in the middle. Gently break the egg into the whirlpool and the egg white will wrap itself round the yolk and cook quite nicely. After a couple of minutes lift the egg out and that's that. What could be easier?

Well, I've given you two of my little gems and I think that's enough really. A girl shouldn't tell all her secrets! So, if you can't get anybody to take you out to eat, or cook a meal for you, at least you won't starve to death.

AUDREY ROBERTS

Audrey doesn't share Alf's love of working behind the counter.
She prefers shopping, but Alf always seems to get in the way.

ALF'S WIFE AND GAIL PLATT'S MUM, Audrey enjoys nothing more than a good gossip. Though she does occasionally help out Alf in the shop, Audrey's never happier than when she's picking up, and then passing on, the local scandal.

It came as something of a shock to family and friends when she settled down with Alf – hitherto, Audrey had led a decidedly racy life, living with a string of men friends. Even after she married Alf, she had a brief fling with a diet-food salesman called Dave Sparks, and even set her cap out for Jim McDonald. Alf found out, and took some convincing that Jim wasn't after his wife. For much of their marriage, she's revelled in spending Alf's hard-earned cash, and once even persuaded him to buy shares in a racehorse. These days shopping is probably her all-time favourite occupation even though it does reduce Alf to a state of apoplexy.

But age has mellowed her, and leaving Alf for a spell made her take stock of her life. She enjoys being grandma to Nicky, David and Sarah Louise, and her relationship with Gail is much closer than in earlier days. The one person she still finds it hard to get on with is Ivy, and there's no love lost between the two grandmothers. Audrey also has a son, Stephen, who lives out in Canada with his adoptive parents.

INDEX